Mastering Self-Motivation

Mastering Self-Motivation

Bringing Together the Academic and Popular Literature

Dr. Michael J. Provitera

Mastering Self-Motivation: Bringing Together the Academic and Popular Literature
Copyright © Business Expert Press, 2012.
All rights reserved. No part of this publication may be reproduced, stored in a retrieval system, or transmitted in any form or by any means—electronic, mechanical, photocopy, recording, or any other except for brief quotations, not to exceed 400 words, without the prior permission of the publisher.

First published in 2012 by
Business Expert Press, LLC
222 East 46th Street, New York, NY 10017
www.businessexpertpress.com

ISBN-13: 978-1-60649-508-7 (paperback)

ISBN-13: 978-1-60649-509-4 (e-book)

DOI 10.4128/9781606495094

Business Expert Press Human Resource Management and Organizational Behavior collection

Collection ISSN: 1946-5637 (print)
Collection ISSN: 1946-5645 (electronic)

Cover design by Jonathan Pennell
Interior design by Exeter Premedia Services Private Ltd., Chennai, India

First edition: 2012

10 9 8 7 6 5 4 3 2 1

Printed in the United States of America.

This book is dedicated to Esin Esendal, my wife and a writer who writes from her heart in order to touch many people, and to my daughters Janet and Lauren, who provide me with encouragement and motivation every day.

Abstract

The surge of motivational titles flooding bookstore shelves amid the worst economic crisis since the Great Depression is evidence of our society's growing obsession with self-improvement. Recently two areas of growing interest among academics have been positive organizational behavior and psychological capital. While books on these subjects have led to a new understanding of motivation, they have limited their focus to two ends of a continuum.

On one side a plethora of empirical data support the academic literature, while at the other extreme is a tidal wave of self-help books, almost all of which lack academic rigor. The popular volumes ignore rich veins of research, while the academic books pay scant attention to bestseller lists. Both markets seem content with what they get. Scholars read their colleagues' books, while self-help gurus rehash the same old themes and programs.

This book gives equal time to both sides. It heeds to the extensive research and careful conclusions of academicians, and then crosses into the realm of self-help and mass-market literature.

The book's nine chapters blend topics that I have studied and taught over two decades in the classroom and practiced in management consulting. Each chapter invites readers to learn both theoretical and practical concepts, and encourages them to apply this knowledge to the workplace. My goal is to show readers how to master self-motivation. The book thus seeks to mediate market-driven self-help dreams and academic literature.

The following is an overview of the book's contents:

- Chapter 1: Why developing a motivational mind-set is necessary to reach personal excellence?
- Chapter 2: Motivation is broadly defined, including motivational myths and how to avoid them.
- Chapter 3: How to navigate the hierarchy of personal and professional needs?
- Chapter 4: Why leading yourself in a corporate jungle is imperative to your success?
- Chapter 5: Unveiling the secret to high levels of motivation and happiness.

- Chapter 6: How to develop your personal brand?
- Chapter 7: Why positive organizational behavior and psychological capital can create a compelling personal vision?
- Chapter 8: Managing change and continuous improvement.
- Chapter 9: Personal excellence through innovation and creativity.

Mastering Self-Motivation is a concise book that is contemporary and relevant as a popular self-help/motivational book. It includes a wealth of research and experience to bear on the subject of motivation. Positive organizational behavior has replaced the field of "positive thinking" à la Dale Carnegie, which is rife with clichés and *Mastering Self-Motivation* avoids them. The *Mastering Self-Motivation Complimentary Workbook* provides a road map for success that further engages the reader to reach personal excellence. Readers will feel energized, motivated, and inspired!

The target audience for this book is experienced managers and leaders—people whose livelihood is based upon influencing, leading, and motivating others within organizational settings. In addition, expanded audiences will also find it helpful in enhancing personal productivity. Consultants can utilize the information contained in this book to better develop executives. Human resource professionals can utilize this book as an organizational development tool. University faculty can use this book to enhance their lectures and employ engaging discussions and exercises. Finally, students of management and organizational behavior can use this book to guide their efforts toward creating a personally fulfilling career.

This book provides theoretical concepts that can enhance individual motivation presented in a comprehensive and enjoyable manner. It is the first motivational book that brings together the academic and popular literature to bridge the gap between common sense and theoretical concepts.

Keywords

business ownership, human resource management, management, motivation, motivation workbook, organization, organizational behavior, positive organizational behavior, psychology, psychological capital, self-help, self-leadership, small business management, strategy, leadership, and supervision

Contents

Part I	**Introduction to Motivation** 1	
Chapter 1	Developing a Motivational Mind-Set 3	
Part II	**Perspectives on Motivation** 7	
Chapter 2	Motivation and You! 9	
Part III	**Personal and Professional Needs** 27	
Chatper 3	Managing Your Needs 29	
Part IV	**Managing Your Expectations** 39	
Chapter 4	Motivating and Leading Yourself 41	
Part V	**Contemporary Motivational Perspectives** 55	
Chapter 5	Recognizing Your Strengths 57	
Chapter 6	Standing on the Shoulders of Giants 67	
Chapter 7	A Look at Positive Psychology 85	
Part VI	**Motivation and Self-Leadership** 97	
Chapter 8	Make the Change Now! 99	
Chapter 9	Reinventing Yourself 111	

About the Author 121
Notes 123
References 133
Index 147

PART I
Introduction to Motivation

CHAPTER 1

Developing a Motivational Mind-Set

Control your own destiny or someone else will.
— *Jack Welch*

You're always motivated, but the direction of your motivation can shift from moment to moment, so you need to find your true north. Have you ever decided to do something, but your gut feeling was to change direction? That's how your internal motivation shifts your thoughts and behavior. Mastering self-motivation is an important concept. Make any necessary changes now; then you can start developing personal excellence.

Every morning you wake up and do things a certain way. You behave similarly each day because the regimen works for you. It doesn't take much thought to shower, dress, drink a cup or two of coffee, and get on with your day. On weekends or holidays you schedule leisure activities with family and friends. Although you may not pay much attention to your motivation, each behavior is preset, triggered by your thoughts and intentions. Your personal motivation is uniquely yours. If the phone rings and a friend asks you to go to a movie or watch a football game but you have a job to do, you have to decide what's most important. Is it friendship, career advancement, financial security, or leisure time?

Chapter 2 will help you to take control of your future. Here are five steps that can get you moving in the right direction:

Step 1: *Create a vision and mission for yourself.* How do you picture yourself in the near future? What are your preferences for your career? How do you see them impacting the people around you? Are you currently at crossroads? It doesn't matter if you're beginning your adult life or are older. Whatever your age, ask yourself, "Does my life have a unique purpose?" Chapter 3 will help you to manage your life so that you'll achieve personal success. When you create a vision for yourself, you'll wake up every morning with a purpose. Chapter 4 will provide a road map that you can use to guide yourself to your goals.

Step 2: *Wing it.* You have to master the art of winging things. Just get up and do it. When a thought comes into your mind and is right for you, act upon it. Don't let complacency hold you back. Become capable of handling things that arise at the spur of the moment. Rise to each occasion and succeed in everything you do. Chapter 5 will help you to guide your life by a purpose and provide you with the secret to motivation.

Step 3: *Pay it forward.* Surround yourself with positive people. Cheer negative people up. Always attempt to make others feel happy and positive. Chapter 6 will help you to develop a great personality so that everyone will want to befriend you.

Step 4: CLIP CLOP. Incremental improvement is necessary for a successful life. CLIP stands for **C**lear **L**ogical **I**mprovements for **P**eople. CLOP is an acronym for the four functions of management: **C**ontrol, **L**ead, **O**rganize, and **P**lan.[1] Take control of your life so that someone else does not control it for you. In the latter case you may feel compelled rather than free; you also may be rigid rather than flexible.[2] Exercise leadership each day in whatever you do. Organize things before you begin your day. Plan ahead as though your life depends on it, because it actually does. Chapter 7 will introduce a positive psychology that will help you to improve the quality of your life and provide you with the optimism and hope that will allow you to flourish.

Step 5: *Smell the coffee.* You are the most important person in your life. By taking care of yourself, you are, in turn, taking care of others. Give yourself positive feedback because it has often been found to increase intrinsic motivation,[3] which will help you to find your true self. Chapter 8 discusses the changes necessary to find your true self.

To begin identifying your true self, define what you are interested in and do more of it.[4] Feel freedom rather than pressure,[5] and focus on "wants" rather than "shoulds."[6] Chapter 9 will help you in the process of reinventing yourself. You should not be judged by the number of degrees that you hold, the grades that you receive, or the educational programs that you attend.[7] Instead, focus on making your work life more meaningful.[8]

You may work for a company that spends considerable money trying to inspire you. Top gurus command fees of up to $65,000 for a motivational speech. Some companies lavish millions of dollars on financial incentives, T-shirts, or exotic vacations to boost their employees' performance. The trouble is that academic research has turned up almost no evidence that motivational spending makes any difference.[9]

It all comes down to three questions. Are you engaged in your work? Do you know what you value most? Do you have pride?[10] Experts agree that cultivating your character is one of the most effective and enduring ways to improve your health, reputation, career, and personal life.[11] When you become personally motivated and self-directed, you will perform tasks well. Your focus, therefore, should be on enriching your life.

Dennis Waitley, author of the book *The Psychology of Winning*, once said, "I like myself, I really do like myself. Given my family history and my background, I am glad that I am me. And, in fact, I would rather be me than anyone else in any other time in history."[12] Can you adopt this statement for yourself? Are you glad to be you and no one else? Or are you struggling to have a sense of yourself—to know what your place in history could possibly be?

You began this journey before you were born. It began with your ancestors. Somehow your name has carried on since then. How did this happen? Is it just a coincidence that you were born? Do you take it for granted? Questions such as these are at the heart of motivation and will be addressed throughout this book.

Motivation is an inherent part of your nature; it is at the core of your being. At the moment you may be motivated by money and other tangible rewards. The problem is that this type of motivation is short lived. For instance, offer a child a desirable reward contingent upon a particular action or behavior, and you are likely to get results.[13] However, without continuous reinforcement of the reward, the desired behavior comes to a halt. Chapter 6 addresses the reason that money is not as important as you think when it comes to your motivation.

Motivation is an approximate science. Chapter 2 discusses how to deal with your own motivational thoughts and attitudes. One way to weigh the odds in your favor is to look at the great leaders in the world. This topic will be covered in Chapter 6 as well.

Here are a few questions that will indicate how motivated you are

1. What gets you motivated at work?
2. What factors result in your lack of motivation?
3. What do you do for fun that motivates you?

This book guides you in answering these questions and provides important information about your level of motivation. You will find out what you like and dislike and how you can change your attitude toward life.

You have what it takes to be the most successful person you know. Progress is impossible if you continue to do things the way that you have always done them. You must break out of your comfort zone.[14] The goal of this book is to get you to improve continuously.

No one is perfect, and you should not try to be.[15] Do not expose a weakness that others see as fatal; instead, choose a tangential weakness. Pick a flaw that others consider a strength, such as being a workaholic. That way you can selectively reveal your weaknesses.[16]

L. P. Jacks once remarked:

> A master in the art of living draws no sharp distinction between his work and his play; his labor and his leisure; his mind and his body; his education and his recreation. He hardly knows which is which. He simply pursues his vision of excellence through whatever he is doing, and leaves others to determine whether he is working or playing. To himself, he always appears to be doing both.[17]

Authenticity is the behavior that expresses the true self and for which one accepts full responsibility. When you act on the basis of personal integrity, you are being true to yourself.[18]

This book will help you to find your purpose in life. A deeper sense of self-guided purpose will reveal your true, authentic self. The motivational concepts discussed in this book apply to who you are now, not someone you intend to be. It is your turn to carry the torch and take the lead in your own self-development!

PART II
Perspectives on Motivation

CHAPTER 2

Motivation and You!

The world needs dreamers, and the world needs doers. But above all, the world needs dreamers who do.
—Sarah Ban Breathnach

How do you define motivation?

You may be accomplishing things that you would like to achieve, but how you go about motivating yourself **is what matters most***?*

Do any two people have the same fingerprint? No! What truly matters most is how you use motivation as you prepare yourself for personal excellence.

Victor H. Vroom of the Yale School of Management found that the term "motivation" has been used in almost as many different ways as the term "work." He reserves the term "motivation" to identify a process that governs the choices that people make among alternative forms of voluntary activity.[1]

You can take hold of your destiny by understanding that you have free will, which goes hand in hand with the concept of destiny:

> The idea of will implies that people create their own destiny. Humans can dream (fantasize) about possible selves—about achieving some goal, becoming a different person, or doing something they have never done before. Next, they can adopt one of these possible selves as their goal, and then, by coupling such a goal with knowledge of how to achieve goals, can make their dreams a reality.[2]

After you finish reading this book, you will become a master of self-initiated motivation.

Definitions of Motivation

- Motivation is a driving force that initiates and directs behavior.[3] In other words, motivation is a kind of internal energy that compels a person to achieve something. It is a dynamic state within a person that is not delimited by personality.
- Motivation is the psychological force that determines the direction of a person's behavior in an organization, a person's level of effort, and a person's level of persistence.[4]
- Motivation is an issue of direction and intensity.[5]
- Motivation represents the forces that cause a person to behave in a specific, goal-directed manner.[6]

Entrepreneur, Intrapreneur, Motrapreneur

A French economist named Jean-Baptiste Say coined the term "entrepreneur," which refers to one who undertakes an enterprise as an intermediary between capital and labor.[7] Much later Gifford Pinchot III came up with the neologism "intrapreneur," which indicates one who encourages creative employee initiatives in organizations without being asked to do so.[8] A new term, "motrapreneur," is introduced below.

> A motrapreneur is someone who takes stock in themselves and sets up a personalized reward system. They take calculated risks and are determined to stay on purpose with incremental improvement. Their intention is to create a sense of direction coupled with intensity and a burning desire to live to their fullest potential.[9]

In order to be a motrapreneur, you have to be an authentic leader.

> The journey to authentic leadership begins with understanding the story of your life. Your life story provides the context for your experiences, and through it you can find the inspiration to make an impact in the world.[10]

> First, recognize that you have a high level of self-discipline. Then focus on the positive things that you have experienced in life so far.[11]

Next, forge some sort of direction so that you can manifest the necessary behaviors to meet your goals and objectives. Especially relevant here is Peter Drucker's important concept of "Management by Objectives" in his book *The Practice of Management*.[12]

How can management by objectives help you in your progress toward mastering self-motivation? Management by objectives relies on defining what you want to accomplish in the form of your own personal objectives, and it also aims at aligning your objectives with your purpose in life. Once you determine your goals and objectives, you can set time limits for incremental steps in your life quest.

The Japanese use the term "kaizen," which means gradual, orderly, and continuous improvement. This involves focusing on small and planned improvements over a long period.

Drucker writes that "History's great achievers—a Napoléon, a da Vinci, a Mozart—have always managed themselves."[13] In light of this point, you should ask yourself the following questions:

What are my strengths? Every time you make a key decision, write down the outcome you expect. Several months later compare the actual results with your expected results.

How do I work? Do you process information most effectively by reading it or by hearing others discussing it?

What are my values? What do you see as your most important responsibilities for living an ethical life?

Where do I belong? Consider your strengths, work style, and values. When you find the perfect fit among them, you will transform yourself into a star performer.

What can I contribute? Based on your strengths, work style, and values, how might you make the greatest contribution to your organization's efforts?[14]

Once you have determined your direction and taken your first step toward it, you have to decide on how hard you are willing to work. When you run into obstacles and face challenges, perseverance will help you to keep trying. If you face a brick wall and cannot go over it, go around it, under it, or break through it altogether.

Your subconscious drives many things you do and, in many cases, things you avoid. For example, consider the following story based on a laboratory experiment.[15] A frog was placed in a container of water that was gradually heated. Slowly heating the water caused it eventually to boil, at which point the frog died. In contrast, when a frog was taken from cold water and placed in a container of boiling water, it immediately jumped out and managed to live. The frog reacted to immediate danger only when it was as plain as day.

How do you manage your life? Do you recognize danger only when it is imminent? This chapter will provide you with a road map for success so that you can be proactive in all your endeavors.

Right Here, Right Now

Do you seek out positive or negative information about yourself? If you evaluate yourself as a positive person, then you seek out positive information and avoid negative information.[16]

Your happiness should be the most important thing in your life. You want to enjoy every moment of your existence and plan for more of the same. Setting goals can do wonders, but you have to know how to set goals.

Coaches help players to set goals, often making speeches that linger with athletes far longer than the time they share on the ball field. For example, in the movie *Grown Ups*, a coach has a lasting impact on the lives of his basketball players. Thirty years after they won the championship the players were still influenced by him. When the five players were boys and won the championship, the coach said to them at a dinner party after the game that, when the final buzzer in life went off, they would have no regrets.[17]

You do things the way you do because of invisible forces that shape you.[18] This is what the coach in the movie was attempting to communicate. He used an analogy based on past success to encourage future success. The strategy works!

You too may find yourself in a position to motivate another person. Perhaps you will have an opportunity to mentor a young boy from a fatherless home. Perhaps you are a single mother who could use the help of a man. If so, encourage a reliable man in your life to help out with your child's upbringing. For example, in the movie *Courageous*,[19] there is much talk about boys without a dad to guide them; so the fathers, in the movie are determined to have a lifelong impact on their children. Below are five actions that can encourage any fatherless boy.[20]

- *Affection*: An arm around a shoulder, a pat on the back, or a bear hug will convey what words cannot, especially when offered by a man who cares about a boy like a dad. For example, in the movie *The Geisha Boy*,[21] Jerry Lewis became attached to a little orphan boy from Japan.
- *Attention*: Watch what is going on in a boy's life and show interest in him. "Eighty percent of success is just showing up."[22]
- *Affirmation*: Let your words and actions inspire hope. Point out all the successful men who grew up without having a father.
- *Authority*: You can provide safety for a young man swimming alone in the sea of contemporary temptation, a dangerous place to be without a rudder. Be that rudder.
- *Acceptance*: With the permission of the boy's mother, invite him to share in your family life.

Keep in mind that you need to be positive and committed to enjoy life to the fullest. While you are on the right path, you can help out someone along the way and enhance your journey.

The movie *Miracle* tells the true story of Herb Brooks, the player-turned-coach who led the 1980 US Olympic hockey team to victory over the seemingly invincible Russian squad. The legendary juggernaut Russian team from the Soviet Union was beat by college kids at the Olympic Games. This was one of the greatest moments in sports history. In a locker-room pep talk, Kurt Russell, who portrayed Brooks, said that if the players messed up this important game they would take it to their graves.[23] The comment encouraged the players to win the game despite the odds of their doing so. How about you? Do you have anything on your plate that, if not accomplished, you will take to your grave?

Motivation comes in different forms, at different times in your life, and from different people. When it comes, you have to acknowledge it, embrace it, and let it work miracles through you.

What You Can Learn from Ants and Frogs

"Swarm intelligence" is defined as the collective behavior of a group of insects. One company found that ants may have the answer to their logistics problem. Researchers looked at the way ants forage by using simple rules and always finding efficient routes to food sources. When they applied this research, they came up with a new plan to help businesses prosper.[24] Do you find new ways to do things that can improve your time-management skills and efficiency?

In the story cited earlier, some alert frogs jumped out of the boiling water. The others eventually boiled to death. Have you been swimming in the wrong pond?

Motivation Myths

Some people tend to credit the myth that personal background predetermines goals and motivation. If you live in a neighborhood in which many people go to college, it is assumed that you will probably end up enrolling in college. If many members of your family have been in law enforcement, it is thought that you too are likely to end up in law enforcement. There is nothing wrong with that vocation, but is it your career of choice or simply a career of convenience? How can you break the trend? How can you make the apple fall farther away from the tree? Do you have the confidence to go against the crowd when it comes to your education, your success, and your livelihood?

You must determine your own strengths and attempt to eliminate your weaknesses as much as possible while you develop your strengths. The question that you may ask is "What do I do with my weakness?" "Life will give us plenty of opportunities to develop our weaknesses," wrote Timothy Butler. "We will not have the wherewithal to do so, however, if we are not operating from our core strength."[25]

Change the way you approach your life; search for what will inspire and motivate you.[26] Effective leaders know how to motivate themselves.

You can set and reach ambitious goals that may have previously seemed unreachable.[27] With confidence in yourself you can achieve personal excellence. Here are five truths that debunk motivation myths:[28]

- *Money* will not always or primarily motivate you. Recognition is the true motivator. You need to feel a sense of accomplishment and respond well to opportunities for achievement.
- You may be *happy* at home, but the satisfaction found during break or leisure time does not necessarily translate into better performance in your vocation.
- *Ignoring conflict* may not help you grow. Not addressing problematic behavior does not help you to improve.
- The notion that you just are *not motivated* is untrue. All human behavior is motivated. The challenge is simply to discover what does motivate you.
- *Intelligence and self-motivation* do not necessarily go hand in hand. There are plenty of smart people who have not been able to find out what motivates them. If you are unsure about what motivates you, you tend to get bored or frustrated easily. The result is a lack of interest and productivity.

A motivational guru by the name of Herzberg indicates five myths about motivation.[29] They are that you are more motivated when you have the following:

- *Reduced time spent at work*. False. When you are motivated, you seek more hours of work, not fewer.
- *Spiraling cost of living*. False. Some bosses can still be heard saying that a good economic depression will get employees moving.
- *Fringe benefits*. False. You spend less time working for more money and security than ever before. The trend cannot be reversed.
- *Human relations training*. False. The failure of such training is reflected in many managers' unethical manipulation of employees.

- *Job participation*. False. If a man is tightening 10,000 nuts a day on an assembly line, tell him he is building a Chevrolet.

Here are some more myths about motivation[30]:

- *He is so lazy that he or she does not even try.* Untrue. When you are viewed as lazy, you may not know how to do something the right way, so you shy away from even trying. You may need a little push coupled with some skill building.
- *Rewards produce lasting motivation.* Untrue. Rewards motivate only for the short term. People will tend to hit a target instead of focusing on the task itself. Some negative effects of overusing incentives are that incentives become entitlements, weaken skills, and enslave you.[31] Do things because you want to, if possible, and for reasons other than receiving a reward.
- *Punishment motivates.* Untrue. Punishment only represses, not eliminates, undesired behavior.

You may have experienced carrot-and-stick motivation when you are pressured by someone to do something. Because you are enticed to do things under pressure, you will either avoid the situation entirely or comply only when pressure is applied. In order to avoid carrot-and-stick incentives, create meaningful work so that you feel a part of something bigger than yourself. Create relationships that engage you, and do things that benefit you personally in some way.[32]

Personal SWOT Analysis

SWOT is an acronym for *S*trengths, *W*eaknesses, *O*pportunities, and *T*hreats.[33] Developing your own SWOT analysis can help you to become more motivated. It is a self-diagnosis that you can do at any time in your life.

A personal SWOT analysis will not only help you to pursue what you love to do but also help you to work on possible obstacles you may face. For example, a strength may be "I am very creative." A weakness may be "I get nervous when presenting my ideas in front of people." An opportunity may be "I am attending a national conference, and I can use this experience to make a name for myself in both my business and personal life." A threat may be "While I have a good education, I feel that without an advanced degree I am somewhat underqualified in my career."

Figure out how you can build on your strengths and eliminate your weaknesses. Take advantage of opportunities and avoid threats. Now that you are aware of how you can prepare for personal success, consider the following perspectives on motivation.

Perspectives on Motivation

Happiness: How can you reach your desired level of happiness? After you experience an outcome, determine why it occurred. Then judge the outcome based on your level of expectation. A positive outcome makes us happy; if negative, it simply frustrates us.[34]

Goal setting: The distinguishing feature of motivated behavior is that it is goal directed.[35] Unfortunately some people get confused with prioritizing and goal setting. When prioritizing a goal, you must be able to recognize not only what motivates you to prioritize it, but also what the trade-offs and consequences are likely to be.[36]

There are two classes of goals that you can pursue for achievement. One class is *performance goals*. If you are pursuing performance goals, your aim is to gain favorable judgments on your competence and to avoid the unfavorable ones. The second class is *learning goals*. If you are pursuing learning goals, your aim is to increase your competence by, for example, learning something new or mastering a new task.[37]

When you set goals, remember that when it comes to performance goals, failure outcomes are interpreted in terms of your ability, while learning goals relate to mastering a task and possible errors that may occur in the process of learning. Performance and learning goals provide clues for escalating effort and for varying your strategies in the service of obtaining future success.[38]

If you favor performance goals, you may say to yourself, "If I have to work at something, I must not be very good at it," or "Great discoveries would come easy to me if I were a true genius." If you favor learning goals, however, your effort is seen as something that activates ability and allows you to use it. You may say to yourself, "Even if I were a genius, I would have to work hard for my discoveries."[39]

How do you plan your goals? Do you evaluate them as performance goals or as learning goals?

Intelligence comes into play as you choose between performance goals and learning goals. Intelligent choices will lead to positive outcomes and a certain level of understanding about yourself. For instance, you may regard your intelligence as a fixed trait over which you have no control, or you may regard your intelligence as a malleable quality that can be developed through your efforts.[40]

If you consider intelligence as a fixed trait, you subscribe to "entity theory" because you perceive intelligence as a static thing. In contrast, if you consider intelligence as a dynamic characteristic that can be increased, you subscribe to "incremental theory." Each theory is common and defensible, but both have different motivational consequences. Thus, if you endorse entity theory, you may prefer performance goals. On the other hand, if you endorse incremental theory, you will be more inclined to set learning goals because you believe that your intelligence is a quality that you can develop.[41]

Take a look at your motivation and goal orientation. If you feel that you are following entity theory, attempt to change your point of view and begin to perceive yourself as always growing, always learning, and always arriving. If you feel that you are following incremental theory, stay the course and continue to develop your skills and knowledge. If you are weak in an area, try to develop that weakness into a strength. If you have certain strengths, see whether you can make them even better or more expansive.

Your self-concept and goals help you to build and maintain self-esteem, which is an important component of your emotional well-being that includes self-confidence and self-acceptance.[42] Associate with people who nurture your self-esteem; avoid those who erode or diminish it.

The Motivation Breakthrough

There are six ways to motivate yourself: earning praise, competing for prizes, seeking prestige, pursuing projects, aligning yourself with key people, and giving yourself power. Attempt to match what motivates you with what you would be interested in doing. Making that choice creates a sense of ownership and empowerment.[43]

Respond to disappointment carefully when motivating yourself and others because expressing disappointment is the most hurtful human emotion. Disappointment is even worse than anger, guilt, and hate.[44] A good example can be seen when Michael Corleone, portrayed by Al Pacino in the movie *The Godfather*,[45] expressed to his brother Freddo that he was disappointed in him. Freddo's life subsequently caved in.

When attempting to motivate yourself, your needs may change, but they will never go away. You may find yourself always wanting more. At some point reflect on what you have and enjoy it. Life is too short to worry about accumulating material things.[46]

You may choose to build your reputation over your character. Your reputation is important, but character is what sustains your self-worth and value. Cultivating an unshakable character[47] will help you to accomplish your goals and objectives. Here are some suggestions for how to cultivate an unshakable character.

- *Desire to become what you were meant to be; become everything that you are capable of becoming.* Steve Jobs was one of the most successful entrepreneurs of our generation. Put up for adoption at an early age, he dropped out of college after sixmonths, slept on friends' floors, and returned coke bottles for five-cent deposits to buy food before going on to found Apple Computers and Pixar Animation Studios. Jobs advises "Find your true passion and do what you love to do. Sometimes life hits you in the head with a brick. Don't lose faith. I'm convinced that the only thing that kept me going was that I loved what I did. You've got to find what you love."[48]
- *Reach for your own personal potential.* Jack Welch, former CEO of General Electric, has said, "Control your own destiny or someone else will."[49] Know your strengths and weaknesses and make your strengths the biggest part of your motivational force. Focusing on your strengths will help you to control your own destiny. The idea that you should turn your weaknesses into strengths is a common theme in the self-help

community. This is a good idea, but it has been taken to an extreme, suggesting that our lives are a checklist of things we need to fix.[50]

- *Accept no limits in becoming better and more alive.* Don't wait. The time will never be just right. In order to win in any undertaking, you must be willing to cut off all sources of retreat. Only by doing so, you can maintain the state of mind that is often known as a burning desire to win—which is essential to your success.[51]
- *Learn to appreciate the small things in life.* When you work, work. When you play, play. Don't mix the two. Give whatever you are doing and whoever you are with the gift of complete attention. On the way to work, concentrate on the way, not the work. Pay attention. Don't just stagger through the day.[52]

Motivation and Ability

Performance can be thought of as a function of motivation multiplied by ability.[53] You have to take into consideration your level of motivation coupled with your ability when you attempt to accomplish a task.

No task can be performed successfully unless you have the ability to do it. Ability is your natural talent as well as your learned competency. Regardless of your competence, ability alone is not enough to ensure performance at a high level. You also must want to achieve a high level of performance. For instance, if you have 100 percent motivation and 75 percent ability to perform a task, you will probably be better than average at performing it. Conversely, if you have only 10 percent ability, no amount of motivation will enable you to perform satisfactorily.[54] This means that you must increase your ability so that you can do your best in all endeavors. It also shows that ability, while it may impact motivation, is a separate part of the motivational equation.

Motivation leads to opportunity. Can you think of a time when you changed your behavior, increased your skill set, or went in a different direction because an opportunity presented itself at that particular time in your life?

Before 1940 the person most often thought of as being an opportunist was Winston Churchill. He had twice changed his party affiliation from

Conservative to Liberal and then back again. However, anyone will tell you that Churchill not only brought courage and leadership to the podium but also saved Britain by engaging Russia and the United States in the effort to stop German aggression in Europe.[55]

Being an opportunist is similar to being ready when "opportunity knocks." The older and more mature you become, the more new concepts you learn. You thus begin to see your interests opening up new opportunities for you.

Individual behavior is motivated by an attempt to satisfy the need that is most important to you at the time.[56] If you want to become more motivated, you have to know what gives you the energy to pursue your dreams. You may conduct what is called a "hedonic calculus."[57] You perform whichever action maximizes the aggregate good, and that action will be directed toward achieving the greatest amount of happiness.

Summary

By defining motivation you begin to establish your approach to it. Perhaps you will become a "motrapreneur" and take stock in yourself while realizing your personal potential. As a motrapreneur you can set up a reward system that provides you with positive feedback after accomplishing your goals, and you can take calculated risks that are challenging but realistic.

In order to focus on building personal excellence, you have identified your strengths, weaknesses, opportunities, and threats. This SWOT analysis will give you a sense of what skills you should continue to develop, and it also will give you an understanding of your current limitations.

Chapter 3 will help you maximize your potential by doing more of what you want to do and less of what you prefer not to do. By learning how to energize yourself, channel your skills, and maintain your momentum, you can further develop your mastery of self-motivation.

Discussion Questions

1. *Looking through recent stories in newspapers and magazines, identify one person that you can call a "Motivator," who also is an entrepreneur. Describe their characteristics and how they may also be an intrapreneur and, perhaps, a motrapreneur.*

2. *What do you regard as your own motivational strengths, weaknesses, opportunities, and threats? How can you enhance your strengths, attempt to limit your weaknesses, prepare to handle threats, and capitalize on opportunities? Discuss.*
3. *Of the myths addressed in Chapter 2, does one or more apply to you? Explain.*
4. *How might the paradigm shift from performance goals to learning goals make self-motivation more accessible? Could it make your motivational process easier? Discuss.*

Teaching Tools and Exercises

1. *Motivation at work*: Motivational right and wrong. Have participants write their motivational "rights" on one board or easel and their motivational "wrongs" on another. Motivational rights would be things that are good about motivating oneself and others, while motivational wrongs are things that may be perceived as motivational wrongs. This exercise can also be done with yellow sticky pads as small groups identify their underlying themes in a collective set of motivational points of view. After identifying five or six key themes, participants can be asked to identify the one key theme that distinguishes people that are more motivated from those who are not motivated.
2. *Motivational bookshelf*: *True North* by Bill George. George points out that that there is no single way to become an ideal leader. Finding your own true north can identify how you can better lead and motivate yourself.
3. *Read and discuss*: Eric Bonabeau and Christopher Meyer, *Swarm Intelligence: A Whole New Way to Think About Business*, Harvard Business Review (May, 2001).
4. *Debate the following*: Money is the true motivator.
   Divide the group into two teams:

   - Team I: Money is a true motivator.
   - Team II: Money is not a true motivator.

   Allow 20 min for this exercise.

5. Getting acquainted ICE BREAKER.

   Have participants respond to the following:

   - Describe the best motivator from a novel or movie.
   - Identify a favorite motivational quotation.
   - Describe the best motivator that you have ever known.
   - Create a visual picture of how you view motivation.
   - Tell us about your best motivational experience.

Movies and Entertainment

A Strategic Point of View

Select scenes from the movie *Patterns*. *Patterns* is a 1956 film by Rod Serling who wrote the original story and screenplay. The movie was originally telecast on January 12, 1955, on the Kraft Television Theatre.

Ask participants to relate motivational concepts identified in the movie by applying them to scenarios, or undercurrents, conflicts, and tensions. The main characters in the story are all attempting to work together, but what is holding them back? Is it money, networks, working conditions, or motivation? What is the problem? Why is the character portrayed by the protagonist being held back and how does that person break through oppression? What perspective on motivation did the Chief Executive, Senior Vice President, and Vice President have? Did they encourage camaraderie among coworkers or did they create a sense of competition? Look for management issues such as ethical or un-ethical behavior, social responsibility or a lack of it, or any other organizational behavior issue that you may feel inclined to write about.

The three main characters are Ramsey, Briggs, and Staples. From a strategic perspective, was the company mission and vision communicated well by Ramsey? Was Staples prepared for his introduction to this board of high-powered corporate leaders? Does he find his ethics and ambition at odds?

Motivational Case for Analysis

Social Media Makes Ink Obsolete

Jack was a supervisor at a newspaper company in Canada. His boss told him, "Jack, you have five days to fire the entire department." Jack knew that health care was not a problem because Canada had socialized medicine, but people counted on the company to be successful and take them along for the ride. Jack had no choice. He negotiated a severance package that lasted up to sixteen weeks, something unheard of in the industry. However, Jack knew that people would still resent him for letting them down.

Jack immediately wrote down what he needed—a friend in the industry who at least temporarily could take on his staff as he let them go. He developed a way to accomplish this task. He contacted all the friends he had met during his forty-year career in newspaper publishing. Jack soon discovered 12 jobs located within a sixty-seven-mile radius. He knew that the obstacles he faced were real because uprooting people from their neighborhoods in a stagnant housing market would be challenging. Also, matching the personalities of workers who had just lost their jobs and might lack trust in their new bosses was also a concern. However, Jack wrote on his to-do-list, "I will accomplish this task and overcome the obstacles." Notice that Jack promptly evaluated his options and moved forward with a creative plan.

For the next five days Jack reviewed the résumés of his 12 staff members, identified their strengths and weaknesses, and matched them up with their new bosses. Jack met with the new employers to ensure that they would help him in this endeavor. They all supported Jack's efforts. He then met with each employee and said, "We are considering phasing out your current job with us. If I can provide you with another position at a comparable salary with a competitor, would you be interested?" Each employee felt that Jack disliked their work or just wanted them out for some reason. However, Jack persuaded them to consider the new job before they jumped to conclusions. Half of the staff agreed, and the other half refused to trust Jack. So Jack decided to hold a meeting. This is what he said:

> Because of reorganization and layoffs here, each of you has been selected for alternative opportunities in the industry. Some of you

may be okay with this, while others may be uncomfortable with our offering to help you in securing another job after the layoff. I have to be honest with you. I have been told to dissolve the department because new technology has superseded our department. According to Angela Provitera-McGlynn's book titled *Teaching Today's College Students*,[58] the tech-savvy generation's ability to respond to visual images and move between the real and the virtual means that we rely much less on reading. This is a problem because more people are moving away from print newspapers to electronic sources of information. Therefore, we are no longer competitive in the newspaper business. Since I had only five days to let you go, I took it upon myself to attempt to help you manage your career. If you would like to pursue the opportunities that I have set up, please let me know. Friday will be your last day here, and we expect you to finish out the week in your current position. A severance package of sixteen weeks is all that I can negotiate with our president and chief executive officer. You all have decisions to make, and I just want you to know that I will be here to support you as you decide.

After the meeting came to an end, the 12 staff members were left to discuss among themselves what had just transpired. They knew that their choices were important and that they had to come up with a decision right away. How do you persuade employees to consider new positions with competitors, and how do you convince your competitors to consider hiring them?

Here are some questions to ponder about:

1. Did Jack follow the self-initiated motivation process?
2. If you were one of the employees faced with this decision, what would you do?
3. Was Jack concerned more about his reputation than his staff members?

PART III
Personal and Professional Needs

CHAPTER 3

Managing Your Needs

If you plan on being anything less than you are capable of being, you will probably be unhappy all the days of your life.

—*Abraham Maslow*

Managing your needs will benefit not only you but also everyone around you. When you have a sense of accomplishment, you immediately feel good about yourself and the people with whom you engage. However, you have to consider both your professional and social needs so that you are not always trying to do everything yourself. Otherwise you may find yourself in a rat race trying to win, and "even if you win the rat race, you're still a rat."[1] If you do not care for yourself, who else will?

In Chapter 2 you learned about motivation and how it may be helpful if put into the proper context. A brief introduction to what is called "need theory" may put you on the way to a better understanding of yourself.

Motivational theory may appear to be common sense, but unfortunately many people do not commonly practice it. Consider Walt Disney's *Winnie the Pooh*.[2] Winnie often puts honey above all other needs. He is motivated to seek, find, and enjoy honey, which is his overriding passion.

How about you? Have you selected one thing in your life to which you devote all your energy? Is there something to which you cling? If so, you are not alone. Many people cling to a habit, whether it is good or bad.

Sometimes your habits are formed as a result of your DNA; at other times it is because of an overwhelming desire to acquire something. "You become what you think about."[3] For example, a rat that found its way to a barbeque after a picnic found some scraps of food that satisfied its hunger. No matter what the picnickers did to prevent it, the rat always got into the grill. Why did this happen? What was on the mind of the rat 24 hours a day? Correct, the barbeque grill.

Need theory provides proven motivational milestones that can help you become more successful. For some people ego gratification is the dominant theme, and life becomes an incessant quest for personal glory and gratification. This type of person soaks up as much pleasure and achieves as much power as possible. "One does not need to be an Adolf Hitler or an Al Capone to be an ego-gratified person," said R. P. Cavalier. "Sometimes very average people are marked as cunning, as ruthless, or as someone that has an inordinate need for pleasure that clearly characterizes them as ego-gratified people. They see no point in honesty or in charity ... It is natural to enjoy a certain degree of praise and recognition. A pat on the back does us all good. The issue is one of degree and reeducation when ego gratification becomes the be-all and end-all of existence. The Latin poet Horace gave us the following advice: 'modus in rebus'—moderation in all things."[4]

Abraham Maslow's Need Model of Motivation

Abraham Maslow, born in 1908, was one of the original thinkers about human motivation. He came up with a model called "Maslow's Hierarchy of Needs" that emphasized satisfying needs to reap success in life. His theory indicated that, by ascertaining higher level needs such as self-actualization, you can become everything that you are capable of becoming. Lower level needs such as food, shelter, and clothing, however, must be satisfied before higher level needs can be considered important. Maslow also maintained that when you get to the growth levels of motivation you have arrived.[5]

Maslow's hierarchy of five needs summarized below, conceived of them as forming a pyramid.[6]

- *Self-actualization*: education, religion, hobbies, personal growth, and satisfaction
- *Belongingness*: approval of family, friends, and community, a loving relationship
- *Esteem*: recognition by family, friends, and community, self-esteem
- *Safety*: freedom from threats of harm, stability, security
- *Physiological*: food, oxygen, water, sleep

His theory was based on the premise of a satisfaction—progression process that one can manage by ascertaining one's needs. Motivation, therefore, assumes importance only as one need is satisfied and the next becomes operative. Maslow believed that the basic physiological needs must be met first before one can address the belongingness needs. The growth needs involve self-esteem (e.g., nice car, career status), but the ultimate growth need is self-actualization (e.g., becoming yourself, reaching your peak level of success, being creative and innovative).[7]

By understanding where you are in the hierarchy, you can determine your current and future needs. Maslow's model can help you remove obstacles that prevent you from achieving personal success. For example, if you are facing a situation in which you have to relocate with the current job to a different location, you can establish a temporary residence so that you can focus on the job and not be concerned about where you will live while working at your new location. By focusing on the right need, you can stay on track while considering different types of needs that you may have in the future. By recognizing that there are motivational implications when pursuing self-actualization, you can begin to come up with a personal motivational strategy to help you reach personal excellence and master self-motivation.

Maslow provided a popular model of human motivation, one that you should understand, use, and apply. However, some have argued that Maslow's schema fails the test of a good theoretical foundation.[8]

> Although it offers an appealing intuitive, logical, interesting explanation of human motivated behavior, the theory as articulated does not appear to be testable. For example, Maslow failed to provide sufficient insight into many different facets of his theory, such as when and where food and water satisfies a physiological as opposed to a safety need, when growth and development fulfill the esteem as opposed to the self-actualization need, where the divide is between the social and self-esteem needs. He failed to provide an exact conceptual definition of self-actualization.[9]

Furthermore, scholars have maintained that Maslow's explanations and conclusions are not considered valid even after 60 years of further research.[10] Theoretical concepts such as validity and reliability are lacking in Maslow's model and, therefore, it cannot be considered a motivational theory. When motivational concepts are theoretically grounded, they can be what managers today call tried and true. "There is nothing as practical," it has been said, "as a good theory."[11]

While criticism of Maslow exists, there are benefits associated with understanding Maslow's concepts. The model is useful for identifying different types of motivators that you may not have thought of before. Motivation, therefore, can be enhanced by making judicious use of Maslow's helpful model.

Clayton Paul Alderfer's Hierarchy of Needs

Clayton Paul Alderfer is an American psychologist who reconceived Maslow's hierarchy of needs by designating the components as Existence, Relatedness, and Growth (often referred to as the ERG theory). Alderfer categorized Maslow's physiological and safety levels as existence needs, esteem and belongingness as relatedness needs, and self-actualization as growth needs.[12] Alderfer's biggest contribution to need theory, however, is his idea of frustration—regression. He argued that when needs are not met in a higher category a person tends to focus on a lower category (e.g., career takes precedence over relationships or vice versa).

Maslow contended that people must fulfill basic needs (physiological and safety needs) before moving on to the next levels in succession—progression (belongingness, self-esteem, and self-actualization). While Alderfer agreed with Maslow's succession—progression process, he added a new concept that Maslow had not considered in his model of motivation. Alderfer maintained that a frustration—regression process is also at work here. When people are blocked from progressing upward, they may regress to a lower level need. While the two theorists disagree somewhat, they both recognize that an individual's desire to satisfy his or her needs is an important component of motivation.[13]

Alderfer's refusal to accept that people only progress up the hierarchy suggests that you need to manage your needs in order to be successful in life. Sometimes a lower level need may become more important than a higher level need. For instance, you may strive for growth and become more self-actualized in your career, but when an unexpected layoff or divorce occurs, you probably will see yourself back at the bottom of the hierarchy attempting just to survive.

Neglecting personal needs may slow the process of gaining success and happiness in your life. Eventually you will attain your goals, but why not reach them earlier so that you can begin to enjoy what you love to do sooner rather than later? Have you ever said to yourself, "If I only knew what I know now, I would have made a different decision?" Need theory helps you to avoid that dialogue with yourself.

Maslow believed that when you get to the growth level of motivation you have arrived. He describes this as a sense of complete self-actualization in which one experiences a fulfillment of spiritual needs and oneness with the world.[14]

How about you? Are you pursuing self-actualization? Do you feel a sense of total fulfillment? Can you project into the future to see yourself doing what you want to in life? Do you have a contingency plan? Have you become everything that you want to become so that you are what you were meant to become? If not, you should.

Managing Your Needs

Take a moment to begin the journey of managing your needs. Write down what you currently need. Keep it personal if you wish. Be sure to develop a way to achieve your plan. Remember that need management is a journey, but it has to begin in order to be pursued. Note the obstacles that you may face as you attempt to meet your needs. Now write an affirmation of your goals (e.g., "I will become a published author by 2015"; "I will finish my degree and become a lifelong learner"). Place this affirmation on your to-do list and achieve something toward your goal, no matter how small, to keep the momentum going day after day until this need is satisfied.

Summary

This chapter covered two important and relevant theorists of motivation, Abraham Maslow and Clayton Paul Alderfer. A familiarity with their ideas is a foundation for discovering your motivation in achieving personal success. You can progress up the steps toward self-actualization, but you must realize that frustration—regression may also take place, in which case you have to reinvent yourself. You then will need to tap into your resiliency to bounce back after a disappointing life circumstance.

Placing ego gratification in perspective and not making it a dominant theme in your life will help you to pursue your needs better. When life becomes an incessant quest for more and more personal glory and gratification, you tend to focus on addictive things that satisfy you. You must learn moderation, reward yourself when necessary, and avoid indulging in things for the wrong reasons.

Chapter 4 will help you to deal with the constant change taking place in your life and the world around you. You will learn the dynamics of goal setting and how you can begin to take greater control over your destiny than ever before.

Discussion Questions

1. *Why is it important for people to control their ego? Do you think motivated people should spend time learning about their ego, or is it a topic not worth discussing? Discuss.*
2. *This chapter suggests that self-actualization is an important quest for someone that is mastering self-motivation, yet some people complain that being optimistic about self-actualization can create significant stress. Do you agree or disagree with this premise? Why?*
3. *What is the difference between succession—progression and frustration—regression and the motivational models of motivation (i.e., Maslow's and Alderfer's)?*

Teaching Tools and Exercises

1. *Motivation at work*: Go to the "Marshmallow Challenge" by Tom Wujec. Follow the instructions to create the Marshmallow Challenge in your workplace. The Marshmallow Challenge is a remarkably fun and instructive design exercise that encourages teams to *experience* simple but profound lessons in collaboration, innovation, and creativity. The motivational component of the challenge is not only the competitive experience but also the fact that incentives plus low skills

does not equal success while incentives plus high skills equals high success. Make a point of this finding, show the video or power point slides found on the website, and discuss the challenge with the group.
2. *Motivational bookshelf*: *Winning* by Jack Welch. Inspired by his audiences and their hunger for straightforward guidance, Welch has written both a philosophical and pragmatic book. It clearly lays out the answers to the most difficult questions people face both on and off the job. Comment on how winning has had an impact on your self-motivation and personal excellence.
3. *Read and discuss*: Tim Brown, *Design Thinking*, Harvard Business Review (June, 2008).

Movies and Entertainment

A Strategic Point of View

Select scenes from the movie *Gung Ho*. *Gung Ho* is a 1986 Ron Howard comedy film, released by Paramount Pictures.

Ask participants to relate motivational concepts identified in the movie by applying them to scenarios, or undercurrents, conflicts, and tensions. The main characters in the story are all attempting to work together but what is holding them back? Is it money, networks, working conditions, or supervision? What is the problem? Why is the character portrayed by the protagonist being held back, and how does that person break through oppression? What perspective did the chief executive, senior vice president, and vice president have? Did they encourage camaraderie among coworkers, or did they create a sense of competition? What cultural barriers had an impact on their decision making? What was (or could be) the core competitive advantage of the automobile company?

Motivational Case for Analysis

A Case Study: Bill Walker Seeks More Responsibility at Tulane Hardware

Bill Walker worked for Tulane Hardware, a nationwide chain store, as senior vice president for 13 years. Bill started off as a shipping clerk right out of high school. After completing his bachelor's and master's degrees, he moved into the ranks of management.

Bill recently received a promotion to regional director with responsibility for fifteen states. In the past, he managed three stores. This was a big opportunity but at the same time a huge challenge for him.

Mary Follett, CEO of Tulane, called him and said, "Bill, you began at the lower ranks of this organization and did a hell of a job. Just approach this assignment like every other one in the past, and I know you will be successful. Let me know how everything goes in the next month or so."

Bill then asked his administrative assistant for a complete breakdown on the experience, education, marital status, performance ratings, and years with the company for every employee in the regional territory for which he was now responsible. Bill also requested a report on any problems that had arisen between these employees and their immediate supervisors during the past year. He felt that he might not be able to solve all the problems of the past, but that he might be able to address the most recent ones.

After receiving problem reports for each store in his new territory, Bill asked his vice president to categorize each issue. This is a summary of what he received back:

- In total, 13 managers felt that they were stagnant in their careers and unable to move up the corporate ladder.
- Overall, 350 new hires reported that they were not receiving overtime pay for working on Saturdays.
- A total of 23 people complained about their limited opportunity to attend college because the closest one was 75 miles away and difficult to attend in light of work, family, and community commitments.
- A total of 6 managers argued that they kept getting Tulane stock as 20 percent of their salary and that with the volatility of the current stock market this could lead to considerable losses for themselves and their families.
- A total of 3 female workers claimed that they had been overlooked when a managerial position had become available.

Bill sat in his office with his feet propped on the desk and wondered about his next move. Suddenly he picked up the phone and called Mary Follett. "Mary, it's Bill. I just want you to know that everything is under control here. I have identified employee expectations and individual needs; however, I need some time and resources to link them together." Mary responded, "Let me know what you need. Be frugal but comprehensive, and I promise I will get you all the resources necessary to make this work." Bill said, "Thank you, Mary."

Here are some questions to ponder about:

1. Why are there so many problems in Bill's region?
2. How can Maslow's Hierarchy of Needs explain these problems?
3. What will Bill do with the limited resources available to him?
4. What did Mary do that made Bill so productive?

PART IV

Managing Your Expectations

CHAPTER 4

Motivating and Leading Yourself

Don't go where the path may lead; go instead where there is no path and leave a trail.

—Ralph Waldo Emerson

C. P. Neck and C. C. Manz, authors of *Mastering Self-Leadership: Empowering Yourself for Personal Excellence*,[1] put self-leadership in perspective.

> Self-leadership is derived from two areas of psychology, the first being social cognitive theory which recognizes that we influence and are influenced by the world we live in. The theory looks at our capacity to manage or control ourselves—particularly when faced with difficult yet important tasks. The second area of the psychology of self-leadership is intrinsic motivation theory. This theory focuses on the natural rewards that you can manifest by doing the tasks that you like and enjoy so that you can harness the motivational forces available to you.[2]

Self-leadership is the key to personal success.[3] By leading yourself, you can become more motivated.

In *Alice in Wonderland*, the protagonist became more motivated as she controlled her dreams through imagination. The story offers some great ideas for motivating oneself through self-leadership. Each time Alice returned to Wonderland, she had to reinvent herself to carry out the same plan with the same people. Alice had to change herself into a person with a plan, goal, and direction. Does this scenario resemble career adjustments when you had to reinvent yourself to avoid becoming obsolescent?

You too sometimes may need a new direction. In such circumstances seek out a mentor who can put things in perspective and encourage you to overcome any obstacle that may be in your way. Sometimes things in life appear to be impossible, but when you look at them carefully you can see that nothing is impossible.

Taking Control of Your Life

You can become better at problem solving by doing the necessary research or investigative work to keep you on track. You have vast databases of information at your fingertips. Local libraries offer this information free. Do you have a library card? If so, do you use it? Books are free and available any time you want them. You can become an expert on anything you like just by reading and researching as much as you can on a subject. Be skeptical, do not take things for granted, and find your special purpose in life.

The only person you can truly change is yourself. However, the more successful you become, the more critics will appear in your life. Remember that the best revenge against such negative people is your own personal success. Let your critics motivate you to be even more successful.

How do you motivate yourself? One way is to learn theories of motivation. A second is to apply the theories that you feel comfortable with. You may choose part of one theory and part of another or combine several.

Marilyn vos Savant, the person with the highest intelligence quotient (IQ) ever measured, recommends mystery novels as brain builders. When people think of self-creation, they do not normally think they can strengthen their intelligence. Our cultural attitude about IQs is that we are stuck with what we have. However, Savant, whose IQ was measured at 230 (the average adult is 100), believes strongly that the brain can be toned as surely and as quickly as the muscles of the body.[4]

Do you make use of brain builders? If not, you should engage in *cognitive fitness*. Play engages the prefrontal cortex, which is responsible for the highest-level cognitive functions such as self-knowledge, memory, mental imagery, and reward processing. To get the most out of play, participate in games and activities involving risk. Risk activates both reasoning and imagination. Activities such as bridge, chess, sudoku, role-playing games, and crossword puzzles provide rigorous neural workouts. Some corporations are creating facilities where executives can engage their minds in play activities. For example, environments such as zen dens are now available in various Silicon Valley companies.[5]

In addition to cognitive fitness, you should attempt to manage your energy better. Mental and physical preparation can enhance your success. There are four kinds of energy that you can manage: physical, emotional, mental, and spiritual.[6]

Try eating more protein to fuel your brain. Rely on protein bars, energy drinks, and vitamin supplements to keep your mind sharp. Seek emotional support from your friends, family, and coworkers. Ensure that you surround yourself with successful people. Avoid toxic people who merely drain your energy. Join social networks such as Twitter, and seek out motivational people throughout the day.

Reduce interruptions by performing high-concentration tasks away from phones and e-mail, responding to voice mails and e-mails only at designated times. When you are working on a project, shut your phone off completely. Every night identify the next day's most important challenge, making it your first priority when you arrive at work in the morning. Have high-spirited conversations. Seek out positive people and befriend them. Tune out negative bosses, and learn to take the good with the bad.

Do you feel that you are doing things smarter? Interestingly, smart people underperform for several reasons, but one way to avoid underperformance is to promote positive emotions and take physical care of your brain. Negative emotions, especially fear, can hamper productive brain functioning. To promote positive feelings, especially during stressful times, interact with someone you like at least every 4 to 6 hours. By connecting comfortably with colleagues, you will help your brain's executive center (responsible for decision making, planning, and information prioritizing) perform at its best.[7]

In the same way that we have unique fingerprints and DNA, every individual is hardwired with a unique style of motivational learning.[8] You thus should select the types of learning tools that appeal to you.

> The acquisition process of knowledge has both a cognitive and an emotional side, or more broadly speaking a content and incentive side. Reading a book, therefore, becomes instrumental in your

own unique self-development based on your current level of education and knowledge. It is important to consider learning and how it applies to your life.[9]

Learning always includes three dimensions:

- *Content*: knowledge, understanding, skills, abilities, and attitudes
- *Incentive*: emotion, feelings, motivation, and volition
- *Social*: interaction, communication, and cooperation.[10]

Now that you understand how you learn and why you learn the way you do, your next step is to channel that knowledge using process theory.

Process Theory

Process theory describes how behavior is energized, directed, and sustained. Here we seek to explain our own self-motivated behavior as a decision-making process. Process theory maintains that performance leads to satisfaction and that we should make a conscious decision about the relationship among job performance, satisfaction, and the amount of effort we expend. "Events of the day" largely influence behavior; past events are important only to the extent that they affect present and future expectations.

Expectancy Theory

Expectancy theory, developed by Victor Vroom, assumes that you rationally evaluate various work behaviors and then choose those that you believe will lead to the rewards you value most.[11] Such choice is based on the way you perceive the situation at hand. There are three questions that people can ask themselves when they are attempting to accomplish a task:

Can I perform at that level if I give it a try? If you feel good about your ability to accomplish your objective and feel competent at the task, you will have a strong sense of self-motivation.

If I perform at that level, what will happen? Having a clear sense of a positive outcome will motivate you. You must perceive that your performance will lead to a reward at this stage of the motivation process.

Do I prefer or value the things that will happen? This is the most volatile part of self-motivation because, if you do not value the outcome or reward, you will be ambivalent about your performance.[12]

Expectancy theory, sometimes called "motivational force" theory, provides a powerful model to follow. It focuses on your responses to the three questions mentioned above as they relate to a specific task. When you work hard at a task, do you value the outcome?

Vroom presented the first systematic formulation of expectancy theory for work situations.[13] His theory, like all the other motivational theories, may be applied to your personal endeavors as well. If you believe that you can perform a task and that you will be rewarded for your performance, you are motivated.

L. W. Porter and E. E. Lawler expanded on Vroom's expectancy theory by introducing additional dimensions to the model.[14] They took into consideration an individual's perception of the reward's attractiveness and fairness and how that perception affected motivation. They also posited that the ability to perform a task is important because one's effort might not necessarily result in successful job performance.[15]

The main point of expectancy theory is that you must determine which outcomes are important to you and tie your performance to those outcomes. High performance should get you high rewards. Ensure that the connection between performance and reward is planned well. Have your goals set up so that, once they are reached, rewards reinforce all your hard work.

Setting goals and monitoring your performance are crucial so that you have a clear record of your achievements. In the morning, look forward to work because you like the prospect of challenge and achievement. At the end of the day, if things go right, you will value yourself even more than you did in the morning.[16] Structure your day so that you get the most from it. Consider a to-do list for managing your time, increasing your talent and energy, and, most importantly, making the right choices to grow and learn.

Can you change anything in the world without changing yourself first? If your answer to this question is no, you are on your way to personal excellence.[17] By leading yourself, you will be a self-motivator. Be your own coach and self-esteem builder. Here are some motivational strategies that may help you to advance job performance:

1. Capture your interest and feel enthusiastic about the challenge.
2. Be a positive role model.
3. Build self-esteem.
4. Obtain personal satisfaction from the learning experience.
5. Involve your project in your daily activities.
6. Develop an increased desire to persist at a task.[18]

Leading Yourself

Self-leadership is a natural tendency. It is one that you are good at because you have been doing it all your life. The next set of ideas will enhance your capacity to lead yourself.

Start where you are: Chris Gardner, the person portrayed in the movie *The Pursuit of Happyness*, says this in his 2009 book: "Everywhere I have been—down every wrong turn, side alleyway, slow detour, or careening in the fast lane at my own peril—every stage of the journey in what has been my life so far was exactly where I needed to be at that time."[19] Although you may have heard such counsel in the past, listen to one more tip from Gardner:

> Whether you are starting on a brand-new path, or braving new obstacles, or trying to get past excuses and fears that have hindered you in the past, you, too, are where you need to be. What's more, you have every possible resource you can name already at your disposal.[20]

Can you start on a brand-new path? Can you verify available resources to achieve your goals? Continue to develop yourself, build upon your skill levels, and continuously improve.

Change your belief system. You may have become a late bloomer who discovered a new talent. The key thing is that nothing else matters but your current and future success. When you change your belief system to valorize the positive things that you have encountered, you develop perseverance. When negative thoughts encroach, simply let them go.

If you raise your standards but do not believe you can meet them, you have already sabotaged yourself. Your beliefs are like unquestioned commands that tell you what is possible or what you can do. Beliefs shape every action, thought, and feeling that you experience. Changing your belief system, therefore, facilitates any real or lasting change in your life. You must develop a sense of certainty that you can, and will, meet new standards expected of you.[21]

Energize yourself. Remember the "Energizer Bunny" whose mantra is "Keep Going."[22] If you change, everything else will change. You see, the multiplier to leadership energy is you. If you are enthusiastic about what you undertake, those around you will also become enthusiastic.[23] Enthusiasm multiplies energy to produce positive results. Energy is the one thing that dissipates as we age; however, with physical and mental exercise, we can stay energetic even into old age.[24]

A growing body of research shows that regular exercise—as simple as a brisk 30- to 45-minute walk five times a week—can boost the body's immune system, increasing the circulation of cells that fight off viruses and bacteria. Exercise has been shown to improve the body's response to influenza, making it more effective at keeping the virus at bay.[25] Instead of regarding exercise as a chore, look at it as a positive thing to do. Healthy living then becomes a lifestyle for you.

Positive Psychology

Use positive psychology. Jim Daly mentions in his book titled *Stronger: Trading Brokenness for Incredible Strength* that we can find strength even in our weaknesses.[26] The "positive psychology" movement focuses on learned optimism.[27] The way you perceive the things you experience has a direct impact on your motivation. If you look at the proverbial glass as half full rather than half empty, you begin to have a positive approach to life.

There is not much you can do about your weaknesses, although as Daly suggests they too can become sources of strength. However, you may be better off focusing on what you do well and become even better at the things you enjoy doing. Weaknesses may take care of themselves over time. For example, you may not like to make presentations, but over time, by building your knowledge and skills, you can become adept at public speaking. Moreover, cultivating strengths increases your level of happiness.[28]

Positive psychology requires staying power. Consider challenges as opportunities. Be positive and stay on the course. You may have some disappointments along the way, but your destiny is at your command. Here are a few secrets on how to achieve greatness.

Dream. Do you just get through each day, or do you attempt to take something from it that can help you grow and learn? Dreaming requires self-leadership. You can first dream of a stage you want to reach in life and then do what it takes to fill the gap between where you are and where you want to be.

Manage yourself. In the early twentieth century French industrialist *Henri Fayol* argued that management consists of a set of activities that is common to all organizations. This idea has stood the test of time.[29] All over the world, universities, business schools, and consultants teach these recommendations for good management.[30] Fayol's four functions of management are indicated by the acronym CLOP, which stands for *C*ontrol, *L*ead, *O*rganize, and *P*lan. Use these functions to give direction to your life.

- *Controlling* involves establishing accurate measurements to ensure that the quality of your work is up to snuff. Use self-talk to develop the idea of controlling. Here is an example: "*I will apply my leadership knowledge, test my new skills, and use my grades and other milestones to monitor my progress toward becoming a better leader.*"
- *Leading* involves motivating and energizing yourself for each task to see it through to completion. This may be how your self-talk would go "*I will read Harvard Business School articles*

and cases on leadership, meet a few leaders, and talk to them about what it takes to be a leader."
- *Organizing* involves setting tasks and structuring approaches to meet objectives. Self-talk in this case might be as follows: *"I will take a course on leadership at a local university, read five best-selling leadership books, and take a situational leadership training course."*
- *Planning*, by which is meant foresight, involves setting objectives for yourself that are precise yet flexible so you can adapt as necessary.[31] Your self-talk here might take this form: *"I will become a better leader based on my new skill set by this time next year."*

Motivation is a process that begins with a plan, a reason, a burning desire, or a deficit that needs to be overcome. The four functions of management can help you to build self-esteem.

Self-Efficacy

Self-efficacy refers to how you feel about your capacity to conduct your work and how you can transfer that skill to another task when you have to. For instance, if you are doing well as a public speaker, this skill may transfer to a political role within your community.

Your previous performance or mastery of a field matters. You engage in tasks, interpret the results of your actions, develop beliefs about your ability to undertake other activities, and act in concert with those beliefs. Typically your performance that is interpreted as successful raises self-efficacy and that interpreted as a failure lowers it.[32]

Self-efficacy thus denotes belief in your ability to execute tasks based on your feelings of competence. The belief that you can accomplish a task may be real or not, but the fact that you *perceive* accomplishing something actually results in better performance. You also carry over feelings of self-efficacy. For instance, if you can cook a nice meal at home for the family, you probably feel that you can get a degree in culinary arts or even open up a restaurant.[33]

Summary

This chapter provided some new tools for your toolbox. Expectancy theory offers you a way to motivate yourself and others by using the power of perception coupled with placing a new emphasis on what you value most in life.

This chapter also looked at energy as a way of life. Energetic people accomplish more than others. Managing your physical, emotional, mental, and spiritual energy can help you to become more attuned to the interpersonal relationships that you experience on a day-to-day basis.

Leading yourself is an important process that you must master to be successful in life. Many people have led themselves well but lacked the necessary communication to sustain their success. People like Elvis Presley, Tiger Woods, Marilyn Monroe, and Charlie Sheen had it all and lost it, not because they lacked self-leadership but because they did not value communication with themselves.

Starting where you are is important for success in life. Right now, right here, begin a life-fulfilling campaign. It may take a great deal of sacrifice and even a long time, but it will be worth it at the end of your endeavor. Dream of a better future and pursue it. You know that you can do it.

Chapter 5 will show you how recognition can provide the intrinsic motivation you need to reach personal excellence. In addition to learning about intrinsic motivation, you will become acquainted with another theorist who paved the way to happiness for many people. Frederick Herzberg developed a two-factor theory that separates dissatisfaction from satisfaction to help you become more motivated than ever before.

Discussion Questions

1. *Performing at your best is considered to give you a strong sense of self-motivation. Why might valuing the outcomes that you may gain as a result of your performance be considered an equally positive incentive to become more motivated?*
2. *This chapter suggests that managing yourself is an important quest for someone that is mastering self-motivation, yet some people complain that too much structure in life's tasks leaves little chance for spontaneity, creativity,*

and innovativeness. How might a motivated person deal with a situation that calls for a great deal of structure but still requires room for creativity, innovation, and spontaneity?

3. *Do you believe that cognitive fitness according to Marilyn vos Savant is just as important as physical fitness when it comes to being a self-leader and self-motivator? Discuss.*

Teaching Tools and Exercises

1. *Motivation at work*: Conduct a self-motivating and change process for people to think outside the box.
   a. Step 1: Create a time to interact as a group.
      i. In advance, gather the large white paper that is attached to an easel; enough so that there is room for people to stand on. One page per every four people. Have easel paper that you can write on.
      ii. *Goals and rules*: Be very clear about the goals and rules of the exercise. Generally, you want to repeat the rules two or three times to reinforce them visually.
      iii. Rules
         - You must move to and stand in a square when prompted.
         - You must change squares when prompted.
         - Each of you must be standing in a square after each change takes place and you stop moving.

   Conduct the activity by removing a square each time you say move to a new square. This will cause people to bunch up on one square until all the squares are gone.

   The end result will require creativity, innovation, and spontaneity by each participant working together as a team or individually.

   Wrap up with the lessons of this exercise. The lesson in this exercise is that we need to identify the assumptions in our goals and rules (i.e., the real customer value, how we create it, the duration of a transaction, and then find ways to delight our customers as often as possible). Think outside the box—literally and figuratively.

2. *Motivational bookshelf*: *Level Three Leadership: Getting Below the Surface* by Jim Clawson. Inspired by practical ways to stay motivated

while you lead yourself and others, Clawson uses a flexible leadership model to help practicing managers understand and apply the principles of leadership. This book focuses on what managers can do to motivate the thinking and feeling of others—rather than focusing on changing behavior.
3. *Read and discuss*: Jonathan Gosling and Henry Mintzberg, *The Five Minds of a Manager*, Harvard Business Review (November, 2003).

Movies and Entertainment

A Strategic Point of View

Select scenes from the movie *Rudy*. *Rudy* is a 1993 film, written by Brian Martz and released by TriStar Pictures.

Ask participants to relate motivational concepts identified in the movie by applying them to scenarios, or undercurrents, conflicts, and tensions. The main characters in the story are all attempting to work together, but what is holding them back? Is it money, networks, working conditions, supervision, or anything else? What is the problem? Why is this character portrayed by the protagonist being held back, and how does that person break through oppression? What perspective did Rudy's father have on his decision making? Did he encourage visionary leadership, or was he oppressive? What other people in the movie helped Rudy create a motivational mind-set?

How did Rudy create the drive and spirit to overcome his obstacles and achieve his objectives? What were his three key success factors that ultimately led to his success? Do you know the three key success factors for your business?

Motivational Case for Analysis

A Case Study: A Merger and a Management Trainee

Lisa, fresh out of college with her bachelor's degree in Business Administration, landed a job with Mercury Bank during its merger with Argentina Trust. She was excited to be selected for the position of management trainee and wanted to please her new boss, Madeline Herrera.

It was late Friday afternoon when Lisa finished her two-week orientation and saw Madeline near her work station. Interested in learning more about her new job, she approached Madeline and said, "Madeline, I was wondering what exactly you would like me to accomplish in my position and how you will be evaluating my success."

Feeling harried after a day of back-to-back meetings, Madeline replied, "Don't worry. Just ask some of the other management trainees, and if you have any questions I'll answer them after you talk to them." Lisa felt somewhat confused by Madeline's answer yet wanted to do her best, so she smiled in agreement and left for the weekend.

On the following Monday Lisa asked Mark, another management trainee, about her new responsibilities. Mark suggested that she begin by introducing herself to each division head and observing the various functions. Then, before deciding which division she would like to work for at the end of her first year, she should carefully consider the manager's style and make sure she got along well with that person.

Lisa later approached Madeline and summarized her conversation with Mark. Madeline said, "When we all start at something new, we have a little apprehension about our tasks, but everything always seems to fall into place. Good luck, and welcome."

Here are some questions to ponder about:

1. What is Lisa looking for in her new position?
2. Is Madeline a good role model for Lisa?
3. What could Madeline do differently?
4. How does expectancy theory relate to this situation?

PART V
Contemporary Motivational Perspectives

CHAPTER 5

Recognizing Your Strengths

The secret of success is making your vocation your vacation.
—Mark Twain

You are not essentially motivated by salaries, bonuses, commissions, perks, benefits, grades, or cash awards. You expect these things. You cannot motivate others with these types of rewards either, and even if you do motivate them it will be only temporary.

The Beatles were correct in their famous lyric about people's not being able to buy love. Money is an extrinsic reward (one that comes from someone else), whereas recognition is an intrinsic reward (one that comes from yourself). We need both to be motivated.

Extrinsic rewards, while they have a place in motivating people, are not the best approach to motivating yourself. Before distinguishing between extrinsic and intrinsic motivation, you need to be clear about the former kind of motivation.

Scholars agree that financial incentives for work can be motivating.[1] However, extrinsic rewards can undermine intrinsic motivation, presumably through shifting the reason for completing a task from internally driven to externally driven. For instance, your "amotivated" actions, in contrast to self-determined and self-controlled actions, are those whose occurrence is not mediated by intentionality.[2]

You need to be self-managing so that you can tap into your passions and satisfaction that extrinsic rewards cannot offer.[3] Now that you have a grasp of extrinsic rewards, it is time to explore the secret to genuine motivation—intrinsic rewards.

Intrinsic Motivation

Intrinsic motivation comes from self-determination. It coincides with independent choice, with the experience of doing what you want without feeling coerced. When you are intrinsically motivated, you spontaneously engage in an activity that interests you. You are extrinsically motivated when you are influenced by externally administered consequences—receiving a reward or avoiding punishment.[4]

You want to have a sense of meaning in what you do. Does this mean that extrinsic rewards are meaningless to you? Not at all. Intrinsic and extrinsic rewards complement each other. For instance, if you work in a bank, the technical work is very important and should be mastered so that you can keep your job. Once the technical work is mastered, however, you should tap into your creativity and, most importantly, your intuition. When you are working for the sake of creativity and not reward, you are engaged at the intrinsic level.

The interesting feature of intrinsic motivation is that the rewards are in the activity itself. Such rewards consist in the feelings and thoughts that emerge spontaneously as you engage in the activity.[5] This consequence is called "flow," which suggests that when activities are optimally challenging you are likely to enjoy them and have an autotelic or "flow" experience.[6]

Another interesting feature of intrinsic motivation is linked to Maslow's Hierarchy of Needs. Once you attain self-actualization, you are intrinsically motivated. Intrinsically motivated behaviors are based on your innate need for self-actualization, achievement, and autonomy.[7] Therefore, the important component of intrinsic motivation is mastery as you strive to develop your interests and capacities.[8]

Two-Factor Theory of Motivation

Frederick Herzberg was widely known as a Distinguished Professor of Management at the University of Utah and author of many books including *Work and the Nature of Man*, *Motivation: The Management of Success*, *The Managerial Choice*, and *Herzberg on Motivation*.

By investigating what makes people feel good or bad on the job, Herzberg identified two factors known as "hygiene" and "motivators."[9]

The latter increases satisfaction, while the former reduces dissatisfaction. You are motivated because you have an opportunity for growth and recognition and because the work itself is appealing to you. The hygiene factors keep you from being dissatisfied, but they do not necessarily motivate you.

You need to do what you love, Herzberg urged, and the money will follow. When you are concerned about money, it only confuses your search for what is intrinsically motivating to you.[10] Herzberg also found that the carrot-and-stick approach does not work. He thus wrote:

> If I kick my dog, he will move. And when I want him to move again, what must I do? I must kick him again. Similarly, I can charge a person's battery, and then recharge it, and recharge it again. But it is only when one has a generator of one's own that we can talk about motivation. One then needs no outside stimulation. One wants to do it.[11]

Listed below are some examples that Herzberg offers of the two factors.[12]

Hygiene factors	Motivating factors
Pay	Meaningful work
Status	Challenging work
Security	Recognition for accomplishments
Working conditions	Feeling of achievement
Fringe benefits	Increased responsibility
Policies and administrative practices	Opportunities for growth and advancement
Interpersonal relations	The job itself

Herzberg's two-factor theory is another powerful tool that, when applied in the right way, can help you to determine why you feel motivated or not. The theory suggests that the basic things that come with a job—adequate pay, a sense of security, safe working conditions, benefits, etc.—are important but may not be enough to motivate you. Over a period of time, such things become just entitlements and not motivators. What ultimately matters is meaningful, challenging work, recognition from superiors or peers, and a feeling of achievement. You respond well when given increased responsibility, an opportunity for advancement, and a job that is rewarding in and of itself.

Do something you love so that you can live a prosperous and happy life. If you do not pursue this goal in your career, you may have to do so via hobbies and, therefore, work may become increasingly meaningless to you. In this case, your leisure pursuits will become more important to you.[13] Why not embrace Herzberg's theory, make it your own, and watch it help you to achieve personal excellence?

Empowering Yourself

Empowering yourself is not a simple task. Like many things in life, it takes time and patience and may not happen overnight. Here are several ways to empower yourself:

- Get on the balcony. Do not get swept up in the field of play. Instead, move back and forth between the action and the balcony.
- Regulate distress. Let people debate issues, provide direction, and maintain just enough tension, resisting pressure to restore the *status quo*.
- Communicate presence and poise.
- Maintain disciplined attention. Deepen the debate to unlock polarized, superficial conflict. Demonstrate collaboration to solve problems.[14]

Here are some questions that you should ask yourself to determine whether you are intrinsically motivated and thus prepared to empower yourself.

Are you energized about what you do? You expect your work, where you spend most of your time, to satisfy deep needs for wholeness. Your work also should provide spiritual support for your values and your aspirations for personal as well as economic growth.[15] Are you energized because you feel a sense of wholeness when you work? If you lack energy, it may not be your fault but that of the job environment in which you find yourself.

Are you willing to accept the necessary risk that comes with motivating yourself? Taking risks requires discipline, courage, and motivation. You must be willing to step outside the established boundaries and old paradigms in an effort to renew and energize yourself.[16] Courage is a voluntary decision in potentially dangerous circumstances.[17] However, once you embrace courage and face your challenges, you begin to develop this behavior.

Courage, similar to self-efficacy, can be enhanced through the successful mastery of adverse situations, emulation of brave actions by peers, social persuasion, and encouragement by others.[18] Taking risks, however, involves accepting the possibility of failure. The problem is that when you experience failure it is natural to externalize the problem and to blame some factor beyond your control.[19] Taking calculated risks, those that you can overcome with minimal difficulty, will help you to enjoy successful living as opposed to succumbing to potential failure.

> At the personal level, the key to successful living is continuous personal change. Personal change is the way to avoid slow death. When we are continually growing, we have an internal sense of meaning and impact. We are full of energy and radiate a successful demeanor. To have such feelings in a continually changing environment, we must continually realign ourselves with our environment.[20]

Have you realigned yourself in preparation of your next opportunity? By continuously growing and learning, you can foster an internal transformation that will enable you to take on more calculated risk.

Are you willing to make hard decisions? When you make choices, you select the alternatives. Then you have to weigh the pros and cons of each alternative that will lead to the most desirable outcome. Once this is done, make the decision.[21]

Do you care about others more than money and your own self-interest? Some of our most significant rewards come from transpersonal motives such as helping others. Think of a time when you felt particularly good about the quality of your work. What about that time when you helped a colleague write a report or meet a deadline? How did you and your colleague feel then? You need to be engaged in meaningful work that is worthwhile and fulfilling to you. By doing so, you experience a sense of intrinsic motivation.

Are your intrinsic rewards tied to your emotions? Intrinsic rewards are those things about your work that generate positive emotions. To harness intrinsic motivation is to understand these emotions and to amplify them whenever possible. Take time to set up rewards that you desire and link them to your accomplishments.

Emotional intelligence can help you to enjoy intrinsic rewards more often. First, develop self-awareness by having an easygoing sense of humor and a thirst for constructive criticism. Second, develop self-regulation by being comfortable with ambiguity. Third, develop a strong sense of motivation by having a passion for the work itself and for new challenges as they arise. Fourth, demonstrate empathy by considering other people's feelings and being sensitive to cross-cultural differences. And, fifth, develop the necessary social skills to lead change.[22]

Does doing the right thing make you feel good? You not only strive for desirable outcomes but you also try to do the right thing, even though it occasionally costs you to do so.[23] Some intrinsic rewards involve a sense of moral or ethical honor. This cost for doing the right thing should be independent of personal consequences.[24]

Do you have a purpose that you can call your own? Meaningfulness represents a kind of cathexis (concentration of emotional energy on an object or idea) or investment of psychic energy with respect to a task. A sense of meaningfulness accrues when you feel as if you are doing exactly what you were meant to be doing.[25]

Do you have enough information to succeed in your endeavors? Knowledge management is important with the many electronic resources available today. Build a library in your home, consult experts, blog often, read everything, stay abreast of current events in your field, and, most importantly, have fun on your journey of learning and growing. Become everything that you were meant to become.

Do you go with the "flow"? Your success may be based on a match between your skills and challenges. Seek out the information necessary to determine your optimal opportunity for success. Manifest a sense of "full concentration."[26] Once you accomplish this, everything comes together. You are doing what you love, and you love what you are doing. Here are four points about intrinsic motivation that you should consider:

- A sense of meaningfulness prompts pursuit of a worthy task that is worth your time and energy.

- A sense of choice allows you to select task activities that make sense to you and seem appropriate.
- A sense of competence results when you skillfully perform a task that you have chosen.
- A sense of progress comes in achieving the task. You feel that you are moving forward and really accomplishing something.[27]

Based on the rewards delineated above, you can use self-motivation and self-leadership to choose your activities, commit to a purpose, and monitor your competence and progress.[28]

Summary

Of the many motivation theorists Maslow, Alderfer, and Herzberg have been the most helpful to people who want to become more motivated. You have to find out what parts of their theories work for you and what energizes you so that you reach your goals and objectives.

Positive attitudes are an important consideration when you attempt to achieve personal excellence. If you find yourself being negative, you are probably experiencing fatigue, burnout, or dissatisfaction with your environment. Motivators such as advancement, growth opportunities, and recognition provide you with a chance to learn new things and find your unique expertise.

The important thing to realize about Herzberg's theory is that the factors leading to positive job attitudes satisfy your need for self-actualization, which should be your ultimate goal. When you are deflected from this goal, you become, in Carl Gustav Jung's words, "a crippled animal."[29] The next chapter will show how performance and personality can enhance motivation.

Discussion Questions

1. *Mihaly Csikszentmihalyi, born September 29, 1934, in Fiume, Italy, is a Hungarian psychology professor, who came to the United States at the age of 22. He said that "Only through freely chosen discipline can life be enjoyed and still kept within the bounds of reason." This notion*

suggests that a person's sense of meaning of themselves increases when they are doing what they love. Do you agree? Consider this idea; is it logical for a motivated person to pursue his or her dream even at the expense of current financial obligations? Discuss.
2. The chapter suggests that happiness comes with becoming more motivated. Certain entitlements do not necessary motivate people but may eliminate some minor frustrations. How might a motivated person attempt to gain more happiness and satisfaction through meaningful and challenging work, recognition from superiors, and an overall feeling of achievement?
3. Describe the ways in which you might increase your intrinsic motivation.

Teaching Tools and Exercises

1. Motivation at work: Icebreaker. Break up into groups of two people. Spend a few minutes talking to the person next to you about what motivates you on and off the job. Then, discuss what demotivates you on and off the job. Share each other's comments with the group when prompted by having the person share the other person's perspective instead of their own.
2. Motivational bookshelf: *Flow: The Psychology of Optimal Experience* by Mihaly Csikszentmihalyi. Csikszentmihalyi's famous investigations of "optimal experience" have revealed that what makes an experience genuinely satisfying is a state of consciousness called flow. He demonstrates the ways this positive state can be controlled, not just left to chance.
3. Read and discuss: Jeff Dyer, Hal Gregersen, and Clayton Christiansen, *The Innovator's DNA*, Harvard Business Review (December, 2009).

Movies and Entertainment

A Strategic Point of View

Select scenes from the movie *We Were Soldiers*. *We Were Soldiers* is a 2002 film, released by Paramount Pictures. The movie provides a great example of self-leadership and recognizing one's strengths. This is prevalent in the first half of the movie up to the scene in which Mel Gibson (as Hal Moore) is speaking to the soldiers just before deployment. Use discretion on what scenes you want to show.

Ask participants to relate motivational concepts identified in the movie by applying them to scenarios, or undercurrents, conflicts, and tensions. The main characters in the story are all attempting to work together but what is holding them back? What is the problem? Why is the character portrayed by the protagonist being held back and how does that person break through oppression?

How does the leader use education and training as a tool to persuade the soldiers to be more motivated when facing such challenging odds?

Motivational Case for Analysis

A Case Study: John Newman Gets His Yearly Evaluation

John Newman began working at Windsor Cosmetics a year ago and is about to come up for his annual performance review. His boss, Sarah, asked John to come to her office for the performance review at 9:00 a.m. This is how some of the conversation went:

Sarah: "I know you are trying your best, John, but I am concerned about your use of time. You do not sell the cosmetics to customers and give samples away to anyone walking by. I need you to convince people of our products' value and sell more of them."

John: "This is the first time I have heard of a problem with my work. I thought that I was building rapport with potential customers and that they would eventually come back and tell others about our products. I was …"

Sarah: "John, you get paid only $8.00 per hour. Don't you realize that your salary is contingent upon selling the products? You have an opportunity to make 40% of everything you sell."

John: "Yes, Sarah, but I don't want customers to think that I don't care about them and that I just want to make a sale."

Sarah: "You need to get out there and do your best, okay?"

John: "Okay, Sarah, I'll try. Is there anything else you can help me with?"

Sarah: "Yes, there is. I'm concerned about your work schedule. You come in at 10:00 a.m. when the mall opens, but you tend to stay all night. You know we cannot give you overtime pay as a sales representative, and I don't want to mandate a time schedule, but I am worried that you may be overworked at times."

John: "No, I can handle it. Besides, I just had a new addition to my family, and my wife is busy at home taking care of the baby, so my work is very important to me now that I am the primary wage-earner."

Sarah: "Well, I just want you to know that as long as you put in your 35 hours your contract with us is not violated. I am considering giving you more responsibility. Do you think you can handle it?"

John: "Yes!"

Sarah: "Okay, then. I'll schedule a follow-up meeting in one month."

1. How are the controls set at Windsor Cosmetics?
2. How are rewards given?
3. Is autonomy given to John?

CHAPTER 6

Standing on the Shoulders of Giants

If you don't know what the end result is supposed to look like, you can't get there.

—*Vince Lombardi*

Believing in yourself is important because no one cares about you more than yourself. Sometimes you will get distracted when negative notions from the past remind you that you are not perfect, but you know that you have the perseverance to keep on keeping on. When you believe in yourself and realize your natural potential, the sky is the limit.[1] If you do not take care of yourself, who else will?

When some type of trauma from the past creeps into your consciousness, tell yourself that you want to move beyond these negative thoughts and place an X over them in your mind. If negative thinking continues to be a problem, you can try this technique. When the image pops into your head, imagine a big red X over it and say "Stop" or "Cancel" out loud. Remember that what you are focused on tends to manifest itself in your life, so take control of the negative thinking and do some positive "daydreaming" about what you want instead.[2]

Your Personality is Your Brand

Although your personality is 55 percent genetics, you can learn a lot about your personality and motivation.[3] Your locus of control, for example, is an important component of how you perceive the world. If you have an internal locus, you feel in control of events. An external locus indicates that you see other people as having control over you.[4]

If you have an internal locus, you recognize that you have the capacity to control your own destiny and are motivated to do so. If you have an external locus of control, you will defer to others when it comes to motivation. You will only be motivated when you feel that someone needs something from you, as opposed to being self-motivated and envisioning your own success.

"The Scorpion and the Frog" offers great insight into the locus of control. When the frog and the scorpion came to the river at the same time, the scorpion asked whether the frog could help him to cross the river. The frog objected because scorpions sting frogs, and for that reason he would not offer assistance. The scorpion replied that he would not sting the frog because then they both would drown. Hearing this logic, the frog agreed. The scorpion hopped on, and, sure enough, halfway across the river the scorpion stung the frog. As the frog was drowning, he said to the scorpion, "Why did you do that?" The scorpion answered, "Because I am a scorpion, and it is in my nature to sting frogs." They both drowned.[5]

The frog had an external locus of control and placed its entire trust in the scorpion. Do you find yourself waiting for someone else to do something or make a decision for you that you can make yourself? Do you ever find yourself placing your own well-being in someone else's hands? If so, you may have an external locus of control. The scorpion, in contrast, had an internal locus of control and took responsibility for its actions. Do you take responsibility for your actions? Are you in control of your destiny? If so, you too have an internal locus of control. When used wisely, this personality characteristic can help you to become more motivated so that you can achieve personal success.

Do you feel that your personality has an impact on the way you perceive your own motivation? The big five personality traits are neuroticism, extraversion, openness to experience, agreeableness, and conscientiousness. How do you rate yourself in terms of these five characteristics?

- Neuroticism describes how you experience negative feelings. If you are high in neuroticism, you tend to be fearful, unconfident, nervous, unstable, timid, and hypersensitive to stressful situations.

- Extraversion describes your preferred form of social interaction. If you are extraverted, you are typically outgoing, talkative, spontaneous, active, positive, and dominant.
- Openness to experience describes your receptivity to fantasy, esthetics, feelings, actions, ideas, and values. If you are high in this characteristic, you probably are creative, curious, intellectual, and unconventional.
- Agreeableness describes the quality of your social interaction. If you score low on this trait, you may distrust others and be suspicious, arrogant, aggressive, bitter, or cynical while interacting with others.
- Conscientiousness describes your level of attention to detail and efficiency. If you fit this personality profile, you normally manifest a high degree of self-discipline and reliability.[6]

You want to score high on conscientiousness because that predicts your work behavior across different occupations.[7] In contrast, neuroticism has been associated with low job performance and satisfaction.[8] Are you conscientious? Do you manifest a capacity for self-discipline? Are you emotionally stable?

How can you become more conscientious and less neurotic? You can do so by being more careful, neat, dependable, and less impulsive, careless, and irresponsible. You also can be more stable, confident, and effective and less nervous, self-doubting, and moody.

The other three personality traits can add to your motivation and personal success. For instance, being more cooperative, understanding, and considerate and less independent, distrustful, and confrontational will help you be more agreeable. Similarly, being more gregarious, energetic, and outgoing and less shy, unassertive, and withdrawn will help you with extraversion. Finally, being more imaginative, curious, and original and less dull, unimaginative, and literal minded will help you with openness.[9]

Great American Leaders

To learn how to lead yourself, study the actions of great leaders. They had to motivate people to become successful, but most importantly they had to motivate themselves. John F. Kennedy had great charisma and was one of the greatest US Presidents when it came to goal setting. He inspired effective national change by articulating a worthy vision of landing on the moon within ten years.[10]

Great presidents have a gift of foreseeing the future in light of a compelling purpose.[11] How about you? Can you envision your future and strive to realize its fulfillment?

The first president of the United States, George Washington, was one of the most persuasive leaders. After the Revolutionary War, the 13 colonies were still independent entities, and disgruntlement seethed throughout the land, in particular concerning the officer corps of the former Continental Army. Discontent raged so widely, in fact, that there were talks of another rebellion, this time against the American authorities. Washington took to a church pulpit and with one gesture won over his audience. As he prepared to read his remarks, Washington pulled out a pair of spectacles and said, "Gentlemen, you will permit me to put on my spectacles, for I have grown not only gray but also blind in the service of my country." The audience, many of whom had served with the General personally, melted into tears. Talk of rebellion was over.[12]

The nation's 16th president, Abraham Lincoln, motivated not only by his policies, but also by his oratory skills. He was the greatest wordsmith when he addressed the country shortly after the Civil War: "With malice toward none, with charity for all; with firmness in the right, as God gives us to see the right, let us strive to finish the work we are in; to bind up the nation's wounds; to care for him who shall have borne the battle, and for his widow, and his orphan—to do all which may achieve and cherish a just and lasting peace, among ourselves and with all nations."[13]

Another great American probably would have been president if age had not overtaken him. Benjamin Franklin was in his late seventies when the time came for possible candidacy. One of his last public acts was to write an antislavery treatise in 1789. He also articulated a vision of "moral perfection" that identified twelve desirable traits:

1. *Temperance*: Drink not to dullness; drink not to elation.
2. *Silence*: Speak not but only what may benefit others or yourself; avoid trifling conversation.

3. *Order*: Let all your things have their places; let each part of your business have its time.
4. *Resolution*: Resolve to perform what you ought; perform without fail what you resolve.
5. *Frugality*: Make no expense but do well to others and yourself—that is, waste nothing.
6. *Industry*: Lose no time; be always employed in something useful; cut off all unnecessary actions.
7. *Sincerity*: Use no hurtful deceit; think innocently and justly, and if you speak, speak accordingly.
8. *Justice*: Wrong no one by doing injuries, or omitting the benefits that are your duty.
9. *Moderation*: Avoid extremes; forebear resenting injuries so much as you think they deserve.
10. *Cleanliness*: Tolerate no uncleanliness in your body, clothes, or habitation.
11. *Tranquility*: Be not disturbed at trifles, or at accidents common or unavoidable.
12. *Chastity*: Rarely use venery but for health or offspring, never to dullness, weakness, or the injury of your own or another's peace or reputation.[14]

Ben Franklin was also a huge contributor to the field of management. America was established effectively as a company in which all motivated individuals could become something more than their birth order in a landed aristocracy would have allowed. America became the first country in which the nation's wealth would not stay in the hands of a few privileged families.[15]

Franklin's 12 Rules of Management

1. Finish better than your beginnings.
2. All education is self-education.
3. Seek first to manage yourself, then to manage others.
4. Influence is more important than victory.
5. Work hard and watch your costs.
6. Everybody wants to appear reasonable.

7. Create your own set of values to guide your actions.
8. Incentive is everything.
9. Create solutions for seemingly impossible problems.
10. Become a revolutionary for experimentation and change.
11. Sometimes it's better to do 1,001 small things right than only one large thing right.
12. Deliberately cultivate your reputation and legacy.

Source: McCormick, B. (2000). *Ben Franklin's Twelve Rules of Management.* Entrepreneur Press.

Maslow, McDougall, and Maltz on Motivation

Abraham Maslow's model of self-actualization parallels William McDougall's work on self-regard. As McDougall defined it, self-regard entails the building of a fully developed, unified character.[16] Have you attained a fully developed character that collaborates unreservedly with colleagues and coworkers?

Another interesting theorist of motivation is Maxwell Maltz, who coined the term "psycho-cybernetics." The most interesting concept that Maltz introduced was that of "creating a new habit."[17] Maltz discovered that your "outer life" is a reflection of how you see yourself on the inside or what he called "self-image." From further observations, Maltz found that it took at least 21 days to form a new habit. Since then his theory has become a widely accepted part of self-help programs.[18]

According to Maltz, it usually requires a minimum of three weeks to effect a perceptible change in one's mental self-image. During this period of 21 days you should not debate whether the program of reconceiving yourself will work or not. Persist in thinking of yourself in new terms, even if the new self-image seems a little uncomfortable or unnatural.[19]

The View from the Shoulder

When standing on the shoulders of giants, it is important to reach back in time before moving forward. For instance, harking back to Sigmund

Freud, the subconscious cannot tell the difference between an actual and an imaginary event. The so-called reticular activating system (RAS) is a part of the mammalian brain stem that regulates sleep and waking, behavioral motivation, breathing, and heart beat. RAS's most important function is its control of consciousness. In addition, RAS acts as a filter to dampen the effect of repeated stimuli such as loud noises. Dampening down repeated stimuli helps to prevent the senses from being overloaded.[20]

The RAS helps you to connect your thoughts and intentions with the universe. Freud found that RAS rapidly becomes a matter of habit.[21] Therefore, you can use it to rule out things on which you do not want to focus.

William James, the founding father of psychology, posited that what you perceive as your current interest is what motivates you.[22] James' schema depends on the conscious will, which operates by choice and attentional focus—the ability to focus attention on environmental cues that are relevant to the task at hand. Intentions, therefore, are more powerful than simply contemplating something.

McDougall made Freud's ideas available to anyone interested in social psychology. His concept of purposeful activity involves seven criteria as discussed below.

Spontaneity can lead to a new opportunity or circumstance. According to Aristotle, "Every result of chance is from what is spontaneous, but not everything that is from what is spontaneous is from chance."[23] Did you ever decide to do something at the last minute, or without planning it, and discover something important to you by being out and about? Existence is purposeful; everything happens for a reason.

Persistence can be seen in the story of two frogs that fell into a bucket of cream. One knew that there was no chance, so he decided to wither away and die, while the other frog kept kicking until the cream turned to whipping cream, and he jumped out. How much persistence do you have? Do you burn the midnight oil or get up with the sun and work until dawn? Perhaps you are driven to complete a project that cannot wait until the morning. Persistence at a task, no matter how difficult, is a virtue.

Variation in direction can lead to upward mobility. Reality presents you with many targets.[24] Some may be important for your success but are not as appealing as others. You may choose the target you desire over that which is best for your success. Have you ever been consumed by such a decision that is important for your future?

If you look for a solution to a problem that is "good enough" but not optimal,[25] you do not seek the best possible solution to problems but instead operate within what is called "bounded rationality." Ergo, to borrow Mads Soegaard's neologism, you "satisfice" and seek solutions or accept choices or make judgments that are "good enough" for your purpose.[26]

In some cases, you may reward for one thing while hoping for another. For example, universities hope that professors will not neglect their teaching responsibilities but reward them almost entirely for research and publication. The same thing happens with students and grades.[27] Means become ends in themselves and displace the original goals.[28] Because grades identify the target for which you strive, they serve as a motivational device. Grades, therefore, become more important for entrance to graduate school, successful employment, and parental approval than the acquisition of knowledge they are supposed to signify.[29]

Do you select targets in a rational and logical manner? Perhaps you choose your direction rationally and develop your intensity logically by looking at the pros and cons of your actions.[30] Direction and intensity are important components of motivation, but you must add the third dimension of persistence.

Intensity refers to how hard you try. This is the element you focus on when you talk about motivation. However, high intensity is unlikely to lead to favorable performance outcomes unless the effort is channeled in a direction that benefits you. Therefore, you must consider the quality of effort as well as its intensity. Effort directed toward, and consistent with, your overall goal is the kind of effort you should be seeking.[31] Perhaps you are interested in a master's program but know that you will have to juggle too many things right now to do well in the program. You then may wait until you have the time before you begin. Another example would be that of completing an intense program before you start a family or have a great deal more responsibility. Finally, if you are truly motivated, persistence ensures that you will stay on point long enough to achieve your goal.

Ending upon effecting a desired change relates to how you feel when something is completed effectively. In order to stay motivated when you complete a desired change, you must take stock in yourself. Upon making it to a new plateau in your journey, continue to grow and learn so that you remain motivated.[32]

Lifelong learning should be at the very core of your being.[33] Break away from the norm. When others begin to coast, keep on developing yourself. Perhaps you have an opportunity to work with a great leader during the summer months, adding significantly to your professional experience.

The key to your change efforts is that you should not change just for sake of it. Only change when you feel it is necessary. "If it is not necessary to change, it is necessary not to change."[34] Is it necessary for you to change? Are you changing for the wrong reasons?

Key success factors can make or break your pursuit of personal excellence. Developing the necessary attitude and approaches for your given expertise and then cultivating lifelong motivational habits will help you to reach personal excellence.

Planning for new situations gives you the impetus to become more motivated. Planning is also essential for your personal development. How many times have you felt that if you just put a little more time into planning that things might have worked out better?

Do you recognize the assumptions built into your plans? You can systematically identify the key assumptions that you are making, highlighting how much you are basing your decisions on your opinions and how much you are basing your opinions on your experience. This will help you to identify your plans' vulnerabilities.

To make a growth choice a dozen times a day is to move steadily toward self-actualization, which is an ongoing process. Do you see yourself self-actualizing by doing what you love and loving what you do?

Improved effectiveness in trials gives you a sense of achievement that is much bigger than you originally imagined. This is because your self-concept improves after trials. The field of organizational behavior offers a wonderful concept called "shaping." When you are shaping, your success in small trials leads to larger goals and successes.

Totality of reaction refers to the feeling of achievement after a long period of working at something that is meaningful to you. It is a combination of the other six criteria for purposeful action. How about you? Have you worked hard to accomplish something and found yourself at a new plateau?

One way to develop your ability to succeed in everything you do is to identify your learning style. Knowing your learning style can guide you in how to channel your motivation. What type of learner are you? Take the learning-style survey that Felder and Solomon provide for free and see your results instantly.[35]

Do you compare yourself to people around you, or do you compare yourself to what you have accomplished in life thus far? You are a master planner in the pursuit of your own personal destiny. This is your life, and you have a purpose for being here. Find that purpose, cherish it, and let it flourish. Ralph Waldo Emerson once said, "What lies behind us and what lies before us are tiny matters compared to what lies within us."[36]

Your character is shaped by the way you lead yourself. If you express gratitude regularly and enjoy your daily experiences, you will tend to be satisfied with your life.[37] Are you hard on yourself when you make a mistake, or do you tolerate some minor mistakes in what you attempt to accomplish? An optimist will look upon occasional mistakes as inevitable and realize that they have no lasting bearing on overall endeavors in life. You cannot worry so much about tomorrow that you ignore today. There is never a better tomorrow than yesterday's tomorrow, which is today.

Theory X and Y

Douglas McGregor, an American social psychologist, developed Theory X and Y of human motivation at MIT's Sloan School of Management in the 1960s.[38] If you are in agreement with Theory X, which is on the far left side of a continuum, you believe that you work only because you have to, and you will avoid work if possible. In contrast, if you agree with Theory Y, which is on the far right side of the continuum, you believe that you work productively because you enjoy work.

If you are more Theory X than Theory Y, you may appear to be very controlling over your resources. You may establish strict standards and monitor yourself carefully. In contrast, Theory Y people believe that they can be trusted to do their jobs, and therefore they are less controlling. Theory Y people feel good about directing themselves. In this case, control by others demotivates you.[39]

According to McGregor's seminal book titled *The Human Side of Enterprise*, the main tenet behind notions about the "mediocrity of the masses" is that most people have an inherent dislike for work and will avoid it if at all possible. They need to be directed, want to avoid responsibility, have relatively little ambition, and want security above all. Theory X people thus need to be coerced, controlled, and threatened with punishment if they are to put forward adequate effort.[40]

In contrast, Theory Y specifies that putting forth physical and mental effort in work is as natural as play or rest. Most humans, McGregor argued, do not inherently dislike work, though they are often placed in jobs that give them plenty of cause for unhappiness. External control and threat of punishment are not the only means of getting people to work.[41] Theory Y people work better when they have freedom in pursuing personally meaningful and engaging tasks.

McGregor applied his paradigm at Procter & Gamble in Georgia and strengthened the company by using the Theory Y model with self-managed teams. McGregor configured the plant as an open system featuring the then radical innovations such as communication of both good and bad news and a peer-controlled pay system. The experiment was a huge success.[42] The plant turned out to be 30 percent more productive than any other Procter & Gamble facility.[43] Are you a Theory Y person? Do you look at your work as play because you enjoy what you do?

Maslow agreed with McGregor's theory when he said, "I must help these corporate types to understand that it is well to treat working people as if they were high-type Theory Y human beings, not only because of the Golden Rule [....] but also because this is the path to success of any kind whatsoever, including financial success."[44]

Human Relations Movement

While McGregor enhanced the literature on motivation, one of the most important pioneers of the human relations movement was sociologist Elton Mayo. Together with his colleagues at the Harvard Business School, Mayo conducted the famous Hawthorne Studies in the 1930s at a Western Electric factory outside Chicago. One result was his book titled *The Human Problems of an Industrial Civilization*.[45]

The research Mayo conducted at the Hawthorne plant showed the importance of groups in affecting the behavior of individuals at work. He discovered that the relationships between workers and their supervisors led to a more potent influence on output than any manipulation of environmental conditions. Moreover, the informal associations of a group at work acted as a stabilizer on the level of production.[46] Do you feel part of a team at work? Are your supervisors, managers, leaders, and business partners building a good relationship with you? If so, the positive effects on your work are a result of their personal interest.[47]

Mayo said that "pessimistic reveries" (negative attitudes held by employees that could interfere with their performance) can be reduced if supervisors are concerned about and listen to their employees.[48] You need to seek out a supervisor, leader, or professor who takes a personal interest in your future success. The important thing is that you surround yourself with supportive people and stay away from toxic influences.

Giants with New Shapes

The term "popular psychology" refers to concepts of human potential that purportedly are based on psychology and achieved popularity among the general population. Many authors capitalized on what is often referred to as the human potential movement that began to develop in the 1960s. Arising from the social rebellion among college students during and after the Vietnam War, it was formed around the concept of cultivating extraordinary human potential.

Many authors such as Anthony Robbins, Phil McGraw (Dr. Phil), and Dale Carnegie became well known during this period. You will not see these people represented in management textbooks at universities, and they do not have a place in the academic discipline of organizational behavior. Why? Well, for the most part their methods are not grounded on theoretical models, and scholars do not approve their logic or reasoning. However, there are many reasons for the success of self-help books in the marketplace.

Such books, often selling millions of copies, have one distinguishing feature: readers can recite their major conclusions or recommendations in a few words. Stephen Covey's *The Seven Habits of Highly Effective People*, for instance, presents bite-sized and folksy sayings such as "Be proactive," "Synergize," "Think win/win," and "Sharpen the saw." A more recent book titled *Who Moved My Cheese?* can be summarized in nine words: "Anticipate the need for change and adapt to it."[49] While Covey impressed self-help readers, scholars called his work common sense. However, Covey responded to his critics with another savvy sound bite: "This is common sense but not common practice."[50]

If you want to become more motivated, you might consult one of the best sources from the popular psychology era. In 1956 Earl Nightingale made a recording he called *The Strangest Secret*. Without the advantage of advertising or marketing, more than a million copies soon sold, earning for Nightingale a Gold Record as the "largest selling nonentertainment recording of the record industry." More than fifty years later *The Strangest Secret*'s underlying message—"We become what we think about"—continues to inspire and motivate people. Often imitated, Nightingale's work remains the top-selling audio in the personal development, self-help, and inspiration industry.[51]

What did this particular motivational expert say that has had such a phenomenal impact? Nightingale's advice can be summed up this way: "Decide now what you want. Plant your goal in your mind. It will grow and ensure your accomplishment." Have you decided what you want? Can you plant a goal in your mind and watch it be realized over time? How do you handle your self-talk?[52]

Positive self-talk comes with a great deal of skill and confidence. When Captain Chesley Sullenberger safely landed US Airways Flight 1579 on the Hudson River in New York, he took control and descended rapidly toward the water. Later he said, "I did not specifically think about the passengers, but I knew that I had to solve the problem. I thought of nothing else but the landing. I was sure that I could do it. My entire life up to that moment was a preparation for handling that moment. Once we landed, I said, 'Now that was not as bad as I thought.'"[53]

Another iconic figure in the area of self-help and motivation is Napoleon Hill, author of *Think and Grow Rich*. W. Clement Stone offers this testimonial: "More men and women have been motivated to achieve success because of reading *Think and Grow Rich* than by any other book written by a living author." Pro Football Hall of Fame quarterback Fran Tarkenton in 1987 hosted a TV infomercial that sold the 1960 version of Hill's book with supplemental audio-cassette study guides. Tarkenton stated that he believed *Think and Grow Rich* to be "the greatest formula for success that has ever been developed."[54]

Brian Tracy, another prominent speaker, provides a unique perspective on motivation in his ultimate goals program. Take any 100 individuals aged 25, he suggests. They all believe that they are going to be successful, but by the time they are 65, only 5 out of a 100 will have achieved success. Much of your ability to succeed comes from the way you deal with life. Do everything possible to avoid problems, but when problems come, superior people learn from them, rise above them, and continue onward in the direction of their dreams.[55]

Tracy provides a step-by-step program for goal setting. "Your ability to set and achieve goals," he remarks, "will determine your success and happiness more than any other skill you can ever learn!" One of the most important arguments Tracy makes about goal setting is that you need to follow a twelve-step system.[56] Goal setting begins with a burning desire, such as deciding upon ascertaining a return on investment of 15 percent or higher. The last step is an unswervable resolve not to give up in achieving that goal.[57]

The final motivational speaker who deserves notice is Denis Waitley, described by Simon and Shuster as "the greatest motivator of our time."[58] Waitley shows how attitude can trigger success by exploring ten positive attitudes and their matching actions. He sheds light on the key components of every profile such as control, optimism, and discipline. Waitley says that being a winner involves an attitude, a way of life, a self-concept.[59] In his book *The Psychology of Winning* he contends that it's a tough, no-nonsense approach based on years of documented scientific research. The techniques he espouses add up to one thing—making you a "winner in life."[60]

Summary

This chapter provided an overview of how you can develop an ironclad personality, improve performance, and stay motivated. It behooves you to learn from past experts, seek out new experts, and become an expert on motivation yourself. A few such authorities were noted, ranging from American presidents to academic scholars to self-help gurus. From each of them you can learn something that you can apply to your life. Stand on their shoulders and see how fully you can master your own skills. Attempt to read and learn about motivation every day.

Developing an internal locus of control is important to your success. The chapter discussed five personality traits as anchors for helping you to become more aware of your behaviors. Managing your emotional stability, extraversion, openness to experience, agreeableness, and conscientiousness can help you to create productive relationships with others.

Learning from past psychologists, sociologists, and scholars is a lifelong process. Beginning your journey of self-development starts with your first step toward personal excellence. Programs and books such as *The Strangest Secret* and *Think and Grow Rich* will encourage you to improve and help you to reach personal excellence.

The next chapter will show how positive psychology can enhance your path to success. By developing psychological capital, an increased awareness of your capacity to grow and learn, you can have more confidence in your ability to succeed.

Discussion Questions

1. *Describe how an internal locus of control may be associated with the ideas behind The Strangest Secret. How might a person's locus of control, as described in Chapter 6, influence a person's motivation?*
2. *With the United States and surrounding countries in flux, some companies are finding old ways to do new things. As a motivational technique, does the practice of looking at our past to make a decision for our future seem like a good idea for you? What may be some advantages and disadvantages of this technique? Discuss.*
3. *Discuss whether you believe in Theory Y as opposed to Theory X. How might a motivated person attempt to lead by using each theory?*

Teaching Tools and Exercises

1. *Motivation at work*: Match the American Presidents and the motivational impact that they had on America.

US President	Motivational Impact
1. George Washington	a. We are not enemies, but friends.
2. Thomas Jefferson	b. Nothing is so much to be feared as fear itself.
3. Abraham Lincoln	c. Dynamic Conservatism.
4. Ulysses Grant	d. We force the spring.
5. Franklin Roosevelt	e. Let us never negotiate out of fear, but let us never fear to negotiate.
6. Dwight Eisenhower	f. University of Virginia.
7. John Kennedy	g. A new breeze is blowing.
8. Ron Reagan	h. The Boston Tea Party.
9. Bill Clinton	i. Government can and must provide opportunity.
10. George Bush Sr.	j. Known friendliness toward Indian tribes.

2. *Motivational bookshelf*: Management: It Is Not What You Think by Henry Mintzberg. Henry Mintzberg, one of today's most respected and controversial thinkers on management, has joined forces with other leading business figures to provide a provocative and unusual mix of writing on management. This insightful book will inspire managers of all types, spark debate, and renew their passion and interest in doing what they do best! "Managing."
3. Read and discuss: Ed Catmull, *How Pixar Fosters Collective Creativity*, Harvard Business Review (September, 2008).

Movies and Entertainment

A Strategic Point of View

Select scenes from the movie *The Last Castle*. The Last Castle is a 2001 film, released by Paramount Pictures. The film is directed by Rod Lurie who recalls that when he was a student at West Point, he was told that West Point does not create leaders but finds them. Pressing the point that leaders are born and not made, Lurie presents two leaders that are at odds with each other from the onset of the movie.

CHAPTER 7

A Look at Positive Psychology

Once you begin your journey, it is not what you will get when you reach the finish line, but it is what you become.

—*Zig Zigler*

Every single thing you do matters. You have been created as one of a kind in order to make a difference in this world. You have within you the power to change the world.[1]

Many great people were not considered *bona fide* geniuses early in life. For example, Thomas Edison's teacher said that he was too stupid to learn anything. He was fired from his first two jobs for being nonproductive. Edison subsequently made 1,000 unsuccessful attempts to invent the light bulb. When a reporter asked him how he felt about failing so often, Edison replied, "I didn't fail 1,000 times. The light bulb was an invention with 1,000 steps."[2] He also once said, "Genius is one percent inspiration and ninety-nine percent perspiration."[3]

You may be on a journey to becoming the most successful person ever, but because you cannot predict the future you sometimes encounter temporary setbacks. Don't give up. "Many of life's failures," observed Edison, "are men who did not realize how close they were to success when they gave up."[4]

Albert Einstein, a German-born physicist who developed the revolutionary theory of general relativity, did not speak until he was four years old and did not read until he was seven. An early teacher described him as mentally slow, unsociable, and prone to foolish daydreaming. Later he was expelled from secondary school and flunked his college entrance exam. After eventually completing his degree, he could not get a reference, taking a lowly job as a US patent clerk. However, at the age of 26 he published his groundbreaking theory of general relativity in the summer of 1905.[5]

You too have the capacity to become great. If you think about what you want to accomplish and focus on it intently, you will get there. Think of a time when you had to work hard at something such as completing your degree in order to reap the benefits.

Butterflies are Free

The "butterfly effect," derived from quantum physics, metaphorically encapsulates chaos theory. The theory suggests that every action matters and that deciding on a course of action makes all the difference in terms of outcome.[6] Most of your everyday life is determined not by conscious intentions and deliberate choices but by mental processes that are put into motion by features of the environment beyond your conscious awareness.[7]

The butterfly effect is more than just a scientific principle.[8] It is something we should all be aware of because we create our own consequences daily.[9] Think of a time when you knew that your hard work would pay off, and it did. Perhaps your prior planning, innovation, and initiative caused things to work out the way they did.

Positive Organizational Behavior

Developing psychological capital is how you begin to master personal motivation and change in your life. Bruce Avolio and Fred Luthans define psychological capital as confidence. It begins with having a high degree of self-efficacy to succeed at challenging tasks. You then begin to envision future success, redirecting paths when necessary. The authors refer to this stage as hope. If along the way you are beset by adversity, you bounce back by demonstrating resiliency.[10] Think of a time when you knew that you could do any job to which you committed yourself. Optimism gave you hope, and hope led to resilience.

Avolio, Luthans, and Youssef present another interesting concept called "positive organizational behavior."[11] The positive psychology movement presents a positive approach to organizational behavior.

The concept is based on a need for a proactive, positive approach to the organizational behavior field, that is, one that emphasizes strengths, rather than continuing in the downward spiral of negativity in an attempt to try to fix weaknesses.[12] It entails positive psychological constructs such as hope, resilience, optimism, and self-efficacy—and when combined, represents what has been called psychological capital.[13] The practical implications of positive organizational behavior are that motivational propensities are identified. For instance, people that are more hopeful, optimistic, efficacious, and resilient may be more likely to do better than people with lower psychological capital.[14] Therefore, you need to ask yourself the question "How hopeful and optimistic am I about my life endeavors?" and "Do I feel confident that I have the necessary skills to succeed in my career?" Most importantly, as you face an economic downturn or a turbulent environment, "Do you have the wherewithal to bounce back?"

Positive organizational behavior is grounded in theory and offers a broad spectrum of insight that can help you master self-motivation. However, you may find yourself gravitating to the extant literature such as Ken Blanchard's work, because the concepts are easy to understand and apply. Moreover, Blanchard provides a number of more recent books that appeal to the ever-demanding and inquisitive public. Such books are not rigorously defended in comparison to books in the organizational behavior field. Motivational self-help books have to be well written, enjoyable to read, and must give you a sense of fulfillment. The academic books and journals attempt to meet this need but from a different perspective. Among the academic circles such as the Academy of Management, many academic authors are leaders in their field. Therefore, their work, while appealing to many people, is more scholarly, designed for a less broad market, and therefore may not achieve mass appeal.

Kenneth Blanchard, a motivational self-help writer, has published several books since *The One Minute Manager*. In a recent interview, Blanchard was asked about his views on the role and impact of a company's mission statement on its employees. Blanchard answered that some mission statements would not motivate a flea.[15] In agreement with Blanchard, Avolio and Luthans said, "Average performance is no longer adequate for sustainability in today's highly competitive environment."[16] In effect, we spend too much time focusing on what we lack instead of what we have been gifted with. Consider, in light of that statement, how much time you devote to focusing on your weaknesses as opposed to developing your strengths.

As you begin to develop your personal potential, Stephen Covey's *The Seven Habits of Highly Effective People* can prepare you for a lifetime of success, while Spencer Johnson's *Who Moved my Cheese?* is also helpful.[17] While these motivational books can help you to succeed in life, scholars advise caution. Avolio, Luthans, and Youssef maintain that, although such self-help books fill a significant void and promote positivity, they are based on limited scientific research and evidence.

Given this dubiety about popular sources and "authorities," ask yourself the following basic questions:

- Do you believe in yourself?
- Do you know that you have what it takes to be successful?
- Do you believe that it is all within you?[18]

This approach of self-examination gets to the heart of genuine, independently directed self-help. If you answer yes to these questions, you have self-efficacy.

Psychological capital helps you to understand who you are, what you can do, and who you can become. Self-directed people are distinguished by the five characteristics mentioned below:

- They set high goals for themselves and accept difficult tasks.
- They welcome and thrive on challenge.
- They are highly self-motivated.
- They invest the necessary effort to accomplish their goals.
- When faced with obstacles, they persevere.[19]

Are you such a person? Do you set high goals? Do not take on too much but analyze your situation and push yourself a little. Do what it takes to get the job done and then attempt to do a little bit more. Look for the next challenge. Henry David Thoreau once said, "Go confidently in the directions of your dreams; live the life you've imagined."[20] Lee Iacocca, the former CEO of Chrysler, planned his forthcoming work on Sunday night after spending time with friends and family on weekends. Do you plan ahead?

When you work with passion, you do not have enough time in any given day to accomplish everything because you are so engaged and motivated. Tom Peters, a management guru, once said that you have to work hard on your skills. Just doing an adequate job is not enough.[21]

Motivational and Self-Help Scholars

Positive organizational behavior is grounded in theory and empirical research. Self-help scholars such as Blanchard, on the other hand, based their writings on anecdotal evidence. Admitting this distinction is not to detract from Blanchard's success. Thirteen million copies of *The One Minute Manager* have been sold worldwide, making it one of the bestselling management books in history.[22] Blanchard was one of the first management scholars who crossed over into popular literature to prescribe a method of applying motivational theories to everyday tasks. He also was the first to apply his concepts to both the workplace and leisure activities. Blanchard, however, only mentioned leisure to compare a person's commitment to play as opposed to work.

Motivational scholars[23] based their "psychological capital" theory on the work of Albert Bandura. Built on Bandura's theory of social learning, they included five cognitive processes: symbolizing, forethought, observation, self-regulation, and self-reflection.[24] These processes help you to focus on current endeavors as you prepare for the future. An example would be that of preparing for graduation from a master's program. You can see how you do with your first-term paper, focus on a certain topic such as women in leadership, and then spend the rest of your time in the program addressing that topic. As you monitor your progress, you can regulate how much time you need to invest in the project.

Goal setting, however, is emphasized by motivational and self-help scholars alike. Both groups agree that goals guide future actions and that without some forethought goals may not be met. With established standards you can assess your performance and adjust it accordingly to reach your target objective.

Living a Purposeful Life

Here are some tips that can help you to live a more purposeful life:

- *Miraculous birth*: The race began before you even had a chance to prepare. You won the game of life by having been born, and there is a reason for your presence in this world. Mark Twain once said that there are two days in your life that matter most, the day that you were born and the day that you figure out why you were born.
- *Determination for success*: An underlying force keeps you going. Physically you stopped growing while young, but the same force shifts to your brain as you mature and establish goals for yourself.
- *Luck of the four-leaf clover*: You are lucky to be you. Like what is promised by the discovery of a four-leaf clover, you too have the good luck of a personally fulfilling future.[25]
- *Force-field analysis*: Joshua Lawrence Chamberlain was shot in his belt buckle during the Civil War.[26] Chamberlain later was awarded the Congressional Medal of Honor.[27] Embrace a comparable force-field that protects you throughout your journey in life.
- *Prepare to win*: Winning, as Jack Welch said, will bring a certain amount of happiness into your life. You should have a positive attitude and spread it around, never letting yourself be a victim.[28]

Sid Simkin of Duke University once remarked that many people cannot lead themselves because they may not have experienced failure. Other scholars argue that failure hurts you irretrievably. Evidence shows, however, that when people fail they often rationalize their failures to preserve self-esteem and thus do not learn at all from the experience.[29] Do you avoid failure? What happens if you fail at what you are doing? Can you accept failure and learn from it, or do you rationalize it away?

You have your own *modus operandi* (MO). Kathy Kolbe has determined that your way of responding to crisis situations is predetermined by a unique MO,[30] one that attests to your personal make up and behavioral inclinations.

Equity Theory

John Stacy Adams' "equity theory" relates well to everyday life in that we often compare ourselves to others in terms of a sense of what is fair.[31] For example, when you get a bonus, you are aware that it is somewhat subjective yet want to know what a colleague got so that you can appraise your amount of money. We spend an inordinate amount of time on this type of lateral comparison is many things that we do. You compare your outcomes with other people's in similar circumstances. When you feel that you have been treated fairly, you are affirmed. However, when you feel unfairly treated in comparison to others, you are motivated to correct the situation by working harder or by finding someone else for comparison or by quitting altogether.

Have you ever experienced a situation in which a peer was promoted over you, or a professor gave someone a better grade than you received? Based on your feelings, you will be motivated either to act or to remain neutral. You may even be demotivated because you wonder whether your effort will ever be rewarded. If you feel that you have been treated unfairly, you may attempt to change the outcome by confronting someone, or you may simply leave well enough alone. Your sense of equity may lead to anger or guilt—anger if you feel that others are being unjustly rewarded more than you, and guilt if you receive a reward that you feel is more than you deserve. The latter feeling, however, is not one often experienced.

It may be difficult to comprehend a situation in which you feel overrewarded, but say that you found a wallet with $1,000 in it. You might think that you hit the jackpot or that you should do the right thing and give it back. If you keep the money, you might feel overrewarded and guilty. A recent movie titled *The Joneses* shows examples of equity theory at work in our consumerist society. The title characters had cool clothes, fast cars, and the latest gadgets, but as the neighbors try to keep up with the Joneses, none are prepared for the truth about this all too perfect family.[32]

Equity theory is powerful because it is based on the way you perceive your personal equity (neutral about how you have been treated) or inequity (feeling of frustration about how you have been treated). In the latter case, you usually set new goals to effect change. Have you ever said to yourself, "This is the last day I do this?" This type of self-talk is related to feelings of inequity.

In many movies today equity theory is part of the plot. Look for brothers and sisters who are jealous of each other, criminals who want to be on top, outlaws who say their names to get recognition while robbing a bank, and other characters that want to do certain things because they were passed over, underrewarded, or even in some cases overrewarded.

A Compelling Vision

You must have a personally compelling vision based on conviction. Anthony Robbins, a self-help motivational guru, once advised that you have to start proclaiming, "This is who I am. This is what my life is about. And this is what I am going to do. Nothing will stop me from achieving my destiny. I will not be denied!" Can you adopt this declaration? Do you feel that there are obstacles preventing you from achieving something? Have you begun to design a life for yourself, one that you will be proud of?[33]

Clint Eastwood said in the movie *Magnum Force* that we have to know our limitations.[34] While many people follow this good advice, do not get your limitations mixed up with your destiny. As you master self-motivation, prepare for change and cultivate your creativity. Know when to retrench or stop in your tracks to evaluate how far you have come and what you need to do to finish the journey. Becoming an adaptable person is a sign of intelligence. Manifest adaptability while you master self-motivation.

Summary

Psychological capital helps you to understand who you really are and what keeps you motivated. It explains how you can do more of what you want to do and, in some cases, less of what you don't like to do. Equity theory illuminates why you act the way you do. It also indicates why you respond the way you do to both colleagues and work situations.

Build a team of motivated people who will support you. Teams are not as easy to motivate as one would think. You need to motivate people in your network to share their knowledge and information with you at a time of need. Doing so creates a bond to help you when you need it.[35]

The next chapter will help you to break your personal code of change. It will provide you with a way to relax old habits, change them, and then inaugurate new behavior so that you can accomplish your goals. Motivational change, like all changes, begins with the first step. That first step toward personal excellence is enough to initiate momentum.

Discussion Questions

1. *Do you agree that people have the capacity to put things in motion by features of the environment beyond their conscious awareness (i.e., the butterfly effect)? Can you give an example? Discuss.*
2. *How can you unleash insight and foster positive psychology using positive organizational behavior? How can you make a difference in the lives of your followers to motivate them to achieve results that surpass their prior success? Explain.*
3. *Equity theory seems to be so simple that many people can relate to it. Many people experience situations in which they either felt envious of another at work or vice versa. In many movies, equity theory is part of the plot. Provide an example in which equity theory prevailed in a motion picture that you recently watched. Discuss.*

Teaching Tools and Exercises

1. Motivation at work: "Balloon" exercise—Before conducting this exercise, gather the following materials: medium-sized balloons and a black marker; blow up complete sets of five balloons and place them in their own individual garbage bag; write on four of the five balloons the following: stress, relationships, grad school, sales, competition. Next, select three to five volunteers from the audience to perform the exercise and three to five volunteers to help you. Then ask the volunteers to come up in front of the group and ask them to give you one major goal in their life. Write the goal on one balloon and ask the volunteer to tap the balloon. Have the helpers give the

person tapping the balloon the next four balloons in the set one at a time while still tapping by announcing them like this "This is stress." Once all the balloons are being tapped, the volunteer may lose sight of their original balloon with their major goal on it. The volunteers that focus on their goal balloon are more focused and should be acknowledged in some way. Once the challenge is over, pick up the stress balloon and ask what do you do when you face stress in your pursuit of your goals? After they answer, pop the balloon. When you get to the balloon that may help them with their goal (such as grad school), do not pop it. When the exercise is completed, discuss goal setting and dealing with obstacles and complimenting major goals with smaller goals that can help you reach your objective.
2. Self-help literature experience: Before you began your self-development journey, there may have been one self-help guru that influenced your motivation. Provide an example of how this person influenced your life. How has this individual caused you to expand your educational pursuits or your business endeavors?
3. Motivational bookshelf: *The Innovator's DNA: Mastering the Five Skills of Disruptive Innovators by Jeff Dyer, Hal Gregersen, and Clayton Christiansen*. In *The Innovator's DNA*, the authors build on what we know about disruptive innovation to show how individuals can develop the skills necessary to move progressively from idea to impact. By identifying behaviors of the world's best innovators—from leaders at Amazon and Apple to those at Google, Skype, and Virgin Group—the authors outline five discovery skills that distinguish innovative entrepreneurs and executives from ordinary managers: associating, questioning, observing, networking, and experimenting.
4. Read and discuss: Teresa Amabile and Steven Kramer, *Breakthrough Ideas for 2010*, Harvard Business Review (January—February, 2010).
5. Debate the following: Blanchard versus Luthans. Throughout the past years, motivation has come from many sources. The self-help gurus have capitalized on the popular press, while the academics catered to a more academic audience with only some interest from the nonacademic readers. Therefore, split the participants into two groups. One being interested in the academic literature on motivation and the other interested in the self-help gurus.

Divide the participants into two teams:

- Team I: PRO self-help gurus; CON academic literature.
- Team II: PRO academic literature; CON self-help gurus.

Allow 20 min for this exercise.

Movies and Entertainment

A Strategic Point of View

Select scenes from the movie *Fun with Dick and Jane*. *Fun with Dick and Jane* is a 2005 film directed by Dean Parisot and released by Columbia Pictures Corporation.

Ask participants to relate motivational concepts identified in the movie by applying them to scenarios, or undercurrents, conflicts, and tensions. The main characters in the story are all attempting to work together but what is holding them back? Is it money, networks, working conditions, or leadership? What is the problem? Why is this character portrayed by the protagonist being held back and how does that person break through oppression? What perspective did the Chief Executive have toward his business operations? Look for Management Issues such as ethical behavior or unethical behavior, social responsibility or lack of it, or any other organizational behavior issue that you may feel inclined to write about.

Dick and Jane find themselves in an economic environment that is uncertain and turbulent. They have to make choices that could affect their entire livelihood. Are the objectives taken by Dick and Jane carefully considered? Did they conduct a SWOT analysis (i.e., strengths, weaknesses, opportunities, and threats)?

Motivational Case for Analysis

A Case Study: Betsy and Tony See the Light

Betsy and Tony both worked at Wireless Communications for five years. Betsy was located in Key West and Tony in Orlando. Both locations were flooded with tourists, and the business was booming. In Orlando walkie-talkie sales had increased dramatically, and in Key West cell phones were everywhere.

Tim Warner, regional director and part owner of Wireless Communications, was speaking at the corporate headquarters in Fort Lauderdale. Tim had his secretary, Martha White, come along to orchestrate the PowerPoint presentation and other needs. While making copies of documents, she accidentally left the salary and bonus breakdown on the photocopier.

Betsy had told Tony that she would give him a tip sheet that she used to get people to buy components at the point of sale. She was known for selling cell phones, cases, car jacks, and yearly service plans at time of original purchase. Tony was happy to get the help because his wife had just had their second baby and wanted to be at home with their infant and two year old.

When Betsy put the sheet in the automatic feed, the machine balked. She opened the cover and found the salary breakdown, which she could not help reading. The document revealed that Tony was getting a 6 percent raise and a $15,000 bonus. That was all fine and dandy until she came across her name and found that she was getting a 3 percent cost-of-living raise and $7,500 bonus. She immediately felt angry and disappointed at the same time.

Betsy was in orientation with Tony five years ago and could remember helping him with his presentation skills. She felt that she was a better salesperson than him with her Masters of Business Administration (Marketing) degree from Harvard Business School, an Ivy League University in Cambridge, Massachusetts. Tony had graduated with a degree in entrepreneurship, from Babson College, also in Massachusetts. Betsy did not know what to do. If she were to say something, she would get in trouble because this information was supposed to be confidential.

At the meeting Tim Warner said, "You all did a great job this year, and sales are up in all territories. My secretary Martha will distribute bonus checks and raise notices at the end of the day."

Here are some questions to ponder about:

1. What happened here?
2. Did Tim handle this corporate meeting appropriately?
3. How would you have changed it?
4. What are Betsy's options, and how will Tony feel?

PART VI

Motivation and Self-Leadership

CHAPTER 8

Make the Change Now!

Most people say that it is the intellect which makes a great scientist. They are wrong: it is character.

—Albert Einstein

Breaking the code of change is not easy. You may not want to exert the necessary energy for change. However, energy is not simply a physical thing; it is also an attitude.[1] You must embrace change. Achievement motivation is highest on tasks that you see yourself performing with a 50–50 chance of success.[2] Good performance then becomes associated with feelings of achievement and competence.[3]

In order to motivate yourself and others, you must first understand four laws: (1) we are all motivated differently; (2) every person has a unique achievement pattern or motivational DNA; (3) what motivates one person can demotivate another; and (4) no one motivational type is better than any other.[4]

The Kolbe A index provides a clear indication of your DNA makeup when it comes to motivation. The index not only predicts how you do things but also how you do things best. This is the core of your being that is not going to change.[5]

You have to be ready to overcome your resistance to change. Jim Carrey in the movie *Liar Liar* plays a fast-track lawyer who cannot lie for 24 hours due to his son's birthday wish. When he tries to tell the truth, he struggles profoundly. The movie dramatizes the impact of expected change. Some of us are so challenged by it that we fight to maintain the *status quo*.

Six reasons account for why you may resist change: perceptions, personality, habit, threats to power and influence, fear of the unknown, and economics.[6] Perhaps you perceive that change will show that you do not have the computer skills of colleagues, or your personality is rigid in that you are an introvert and not open to change. You may fear the threat of a challenging new boss or professor. Sometimes we also fear venturing into unfamiliar territory. Or you may be worried about financial resources when beginning a new course or work-related challenge.

You thus tend to perceive selectively those things that fit most comfortably with your current view of the world. You may resist the possible impact of change by reading or listening only to what you agree with, conveniently forgetting any knowledge that could lead to other viewpoints.

Resistance to Change

Some aspects of your personality may predispose you to resist change. For instance, if you have low self-esteem, you are more likely to resist change because you see only its negative aspects.[7] One way to address this situation is to realize that many other people succeeded in overcoming this challenge and that you will too. Self-esteem develops over time.

Do you direct your own life? What happens if you lose your influence over others? In the movie *Rudy* the protagonist set short-term goals to achieve long-range objectives and works tirelessly toward realizing those goals.[8] Can you set short-term goals to reach one of your long-term objectives?

Another movie titled *Patterns* is a great example of threats to power and influence. Master storyteller Rod Sterling's screenplay delves into the mind of an ordinary man caught in the middle of a corporate power play.[9] Have you ever been caught in a power play in which you and a colleague were interested in the same position, political group, or leadership role?

It is important for you to do everything you can to prevent becoming obsolete. Always realize that no one is irreplaceable and that the only insurance plan you have for keeping your job is your individual performance and personal development. Don't worry about things that might happen in your career; instead, seek out the necessary resources to keep abreast. Leo Buscaglia once said, "Worry never robs tomorrow of its sorrow; it only saps today of its joy."[10] Zig Zigler asked rhetorically, "Do you worry about what you can't change?"[11]

If you develop what interests you, you will find your true passion. You have been gifted with the ability to regenerate your neural pathways (neural tracts connecting one part of the nervous system with another).[12] If you are not passionate about what you are doing, if your heart isn't in it, or if an activity does not have meaning for you, you are not going to devote the time and energy required to be successful.[13]

Does financial compensation weigh heavily on your mind when it comes to change? Mark Twain once said that lack of money is the root of all evil.[14] You also may not like to go backward in life. General Ulysses S. Grant once mentioned that he never liked to go backward when he had begun to advance.[15] How about you? Do you like to maintain forward momentum or mind retreating when faced with a temporary obstacle?

Unfreeze, Change, Refreeze

When you make a positive change, attempt to maintain it. Kurt Lewin, a social psychologist, argues that you must tie a figurative knot at the end of your change process to ensure that you do not revert to old behavior.[16] Change toward a higher level of performance is frequently short lived. Permanency at the new level should be included in the objective.

How do you develop the tenacity to stick to your changed behavior? One way is by using Lewin's force field analysis. Lewin approached change from the standpoint of where you are today, where you need to be, and how you can get there.[17]

Lewin's first step in the process is to *unfreeze*. After gathering information on a need for change based on current behavior, unfreezing involves reducing your personal resistance to change. In *moving toward a desired state*, the second step, you channel positive energy in the direction of the change you seek. The final step of *refreezing* involves finding ways to reward yourself for making the change and ensuring its permanence.

Force field analysis is a great way to change a behavior or even add a new one. Knowledge is like lettuce left in the refrigerator. If you use it, everyone gets some to enjoy while it is fresh; if you wait too long, it will wither away and spoil. Take your knowledge and spread it around so that people can learn from you. An example of this would be implementation of the new skills acquired from a course, book, or seminar. The more quickly you convert the skills into real-world applications, the sooner they will become your own.

The movie *Ratatouille* provides insight into the nature of change. Django shows his son Remy the exterminator shop and tells him that this is the world we live in. Remy disagrees with his father, saying that "Change is nature, the part we can influence, and it starts when we decide." Remy embraces change. Is change a natural process for you? With hard work and a little luck, do you feel that you can move forward in all of your endeavors? Your destination is yours. You own it.

Here are three key concepts to consider before you embark on some type of change. One, *envision* a future goal and set some new standards of performance for yourself. Two, *energize* yourself by looking for role models and then becoming a role model yourself. Three, *enable* yourself by making sure that you have the resources to support your change efforts.[18] Most importantly, reward yourself as often as possible to reinforce yourself each step along the way.

Kotter's Eight-Step Change Model

Another paradigm you can apply is John P. Kotter's eight-step change model. As you begin your journey of personal change and mastery of self-motivation, consider the following:

1. Create a sense of urgency.
2. Form a powerful guiding coalition.
3. Create a personalized and appropriate vision.
4. Communicate the vision.
5. Empower others to act on the vision.
6. Plan short-term wins. Consolidate improvements and produce more change.
7. Institutionalize new approaches.
8. Anchor the change.[19]

While following all eight steps in the right order, anticipate common pitfalls. For example, if you embark on a new degree program and find out that your financial aid will no longer be available, you may have to get resources from another source. Planning ahead by creating a coalition of support may help.

It may be hard to leave your comfort zone, but almost everything you do in life has some sort of risk. Staying where you are is just as risky, and becoming obsolete may leave you with limited options.[20] A sense of urgency provides the impetus to change even when you may feel that change is not necessary.

You have to believe that your ideas are unique and, if implemented, will change things for the better. Be sure to let the right people know about your endeavor. Can you honestly say that colleagues will support your change effort? Select only those who will be supportive and tell others about your success later. If you cannot put together a coalition, you may have to go for it alone.

Be sure to show the people around you how you will implement your new behaviors by becoming a role model. Read a book for an hour each day. Create a library in your home. Network with people and tell them what your goals and aspirations are while finding better ways to achieve your goals. Remove things that obstruct your vision. Encourage a little risk taking and beware of people who may come between you and your vision.

Planning short-term wins will help you to break down your change effort into manageable phases for achieving your overall objective. As noted previously, know when you see improvement and reward yourself accordingly, even if it is only for slight improvement. Do not take things for granted. Finally, make adjustments when necessary to keep yourself on track.

Continuous Improvement

Edward Deming, the total-quality-management guru, provides a practical tool for carrying out continuous improvement. The technique is called "plan, do, check, and act."

You can begin the Deming cycle by asking yourself a few questions. What is your short-term goal and how does it relate to your overall objective?

What actions and behavior can you manifest to ensure that you reach your target?

- The *plan* stage involves making necessary improvements.
- The *do* stage involves executing what you planned in light of pros and cons.
- The *check* stage involves making adjustments or even cutting losses if necessary.
- Finally, the *act* stage involves implementing your ideas for positive change.

You can repeat this cycle over and over again to see your short-term wins coupled with continuous improvement blossom.[21]

Summary

The Kolbe A index provides a new approach to motivation. No two people are exactly alike, and you must take stock of your own personality and potential.

Movies such as *Rudy*, *Patterns*, and *Ratatouille* provide inspiration for developing your skills and accomplishing your goals so that you do not become obsolete in your chosen field or profession.

Lewin and Kotter encourage the necessary fortitude to make positive changes in your life. Lewin uses the example of an ice cube for the process of effecting change. One first thaws out the ice, makes changes as needed, and then refreezes the ice or new skills.[22]

Kotter's eight-step process invites you to consolidate improvements and produce more change. He advises reinvigorating the change process through creative projects, not slowing down when you have minor successes, and celebrating the suggestions of colleagues.[23]

Deming proposes the notion of continuous improvement by showing you how to plan and implement your change effort.

The next chapter will help you to reinvent yourself. You will learn how to create a new you, one of which you will be justifiably proud. Chapter 9 will help you to design a life worth living and catapult you into personal success.

Discussion Questions

1. *Think of a problem situation that you may be facing that you would like to change. Describe how you would initiate a change and follow through using Kotter's eight-stage framework.*
2. *How can you reduce your own resistance to change or that of the people around you?*
3. *Continuous improvement coupled with planned change is an ideal state. Do you feel that change can happen in a serendipitous manner? Discuss. Can you think of an example?*

Teaching Tools and Exercises

1. *Motivation at work*: personal artifact: Announce to your followers that you would like them to bring in an artifact and present what the artifact means to them to the group for about 3 min each. The artifact can be anything from something that they received as an award at work or home, family heirloom, children, or anything else that means a great deal to them.
2. *Motivational bookshelf: What the CEO Wants You to Know* by Ram Charan. Charan points out that it is no different to run a lemonade stand than it is to run a company. He feels that the best CEOs have a knack for bringing the most complex business down to the fundamentals—focus on the basics and make money for the company.
3. *Read and discuss*: Peter Drucker, *Managing Oneself*, Harvard Business Review (1999).
4. *Debate the following*: Opportunity knocks, but we sometimes ignore it, why? Discuss.

Peter Neville asks a question as the title of his book *Winston Churchill: Statesman or Opportunist?*

Divide the participants into two teams:

- Team I: Winston Churchill was right when he was noted as an opportunist.
- Team II: There is no room for motivators to be opportunists. Opportunists are wrong when they pursue something for their own gain.

Allow 20 min for this exercise.

Movies and Entertainment

A Strategic Point of View

Select scenes from the movie *The Pursuit of Happyness*. The Pursuit of Happyness is a 2006 film written by John Wiggins, which is based on a true story about a man named Christopher Gardner. Gardner is forced to live out in the streets with his son. He takes on a job as a stockbroker, but before he can receive pay, he needs to go through 6 months of training.

Ask participants to relate motivational concepts identified in the movie by applying them to scenarios, or undercurrents, conflicts, and tensions. The main character in the story is attempting to work but what is holding him back? Is it money, networks, working conditions, or leadership? What is the problem? Why is this character portrayed by the protagonist being held back and how does that person break through oppression? What perspective did Gardner have toward reaching his major goal or objective? Look for management issues such as mentoring, guiding, delegating, encouraging, and most importantly, motivating.

How did Gardner plan his strategy to become a stockbroker? Did he learn lessons from others or teach lessons to his son, if so, how? Strategic implementation requires both a short-term and long-term perspective. Did Gardner realize this?

Motivational Case for Analysis

A Case Study: Creating a Path That People Will Follow

Poem: "The Calf-Path" by Sam Walter Foss.[24]

One day through the primeval wood
A calf walked home as good calves should;
But made a trail all bent askew,
A crooked trail as all calves do.
Since then three hundred years have fled,
And I infer the calf is dead.
But still he left behind his trail,

And thereby hangs my moral tale.

The trail was taken up next day

By a lone dog that passed that way;

And then a wise bell—wether sheep

Pursued the trail o'er vale and steep,

And drew the flock behind him, too,

As good bell—wethers always do.

And from that day, o'er hill and glade,

Through those old woods a path was made.

And many men wound in and out,

And dodged and turned and bent about,

And uttered words of righteous wrath

Because 'twas such a crooked path;

But still they followed—do not laugh -

The first migrations of that calf,

And through this winding wood-way stalked

Because he wobbled when he walked.

This forest path became a lane

That bent and turned and turned again;

This crooked lane became a road,

Where many a poor horse with his load

Toiled on beneath the burning sun,

And traveled some three miles in one.

And thus a century and a half

They trod the footsteps of that calf.

The years passed on in swiftness fleet,

The road became a village street;

And this, before men were aware,

A city's crowded thoroughfare.

And soon the central street was this

Of a renowned metropolis;
And men two centuries and a half
Trod in the footsteps of that calf.
Each day a hundred thousand rout
Followed this zigzag calf about
And o'er his crooked journey went
The traffic of a continent.
A hundred thousand men were led
By one calf near three centuries dead.
They followed still his crooked way.
And lost one hundred years a day,
For thus such reverence is lent
To well-established precedent.
A moral lesson this might teach
Were I ordained and called to preach;
For men are prone to go it blind
Along the calf-paths of the mind,
And work away from sun to sun
To do what other men have done.
They follow in the beaten track,
And out and in, and forth and back,
And still their devious course pursue,
To keep the path that others do.
They keep the path a sacred groove,
Along which all their lives they move;
But how the wise old wood-gods laugh,
Who saw the first primeval calf.
Ah, many things this tale might teach—
But I am not ordained to preach.

"The Calf Path" by Sam Walter Foss is a wonderful poem that teaches the importance of our journey in life. A long time ago a calf blazed a trail that subsequently became a thoroughfare that people used. As the years passed, the path eventually became a village street.

Foss' story, written in the late 1800s, is a parable about change. "It dares you," observes one commentator, "to challenge what is already there and to chart new paths through your daily woods."[25]

Here are some questions to ponder about:

1. Think of a time when you followed the same path that someone else blazed. Could you have made it better?
2. How can you make your path more useful for others?
3. Think of a new approach to your endeavors and consider a fresh perspective for continuous growth and development.

CHAPTER 9

Reinventing Yourself

The world is but a canvas for your imagination.
—Henry David Thoreau

Do you often find yourself burning the midnight oil or going the extra mile? When you are busy innovating, tapping into your creativity, and reinventing yourself, you often feel alone and apart from other people. That short-term lack of immediate connection is a result of your internal locus of control—your ability to control your own destiny. Scott Peck in *The Road Less Traveled* guides his readers through the hard and sometimes painful process of change toward a higher level of self-understanding.[1]

Robert Frost's poem *The Road Not Taken*, the source of Peck's title, shows what happens when you come at crossroads in life and have to make a choice. Sometimes, when you come to a fork in the road, you go with your gut feeling. If you make a mistake, it's okay. Simply be glad that you had the opportunity to make the choice for yourself.

How can you move from impasse to action? When you make an "as if" decision, you have an opportunity to trigger *thinking, feeling, intuition, and sensing*.[2] These are the four domains of consciousness that psychologist Carl Gustav Jung described in great detail. According to his model, each of us is dominant in one of the four, and we "lead" with that domain when we attempt to understand the world and make decisions. Impasse, however, forces us out of our dominant mode, thereby challenging us to use more of our cognitive awareness to select the option that makes sense and feels right.[3] Ergo, impasse can actually enhance action as you use all the four aspects of consciousness to overcome the obstacle that you face.

Reward Systems

Effective reward systems will inevitably motivate you. What do you want right now? What do you need? How can you get it? Can you change some behaviors to accomplish more? If you cannot answer these questions, you are not alone. Mastering self-motivation is an ongoing process. It takes time and includes incremental successes, no matter how small, that lead to personal excellence.

Steve Kerr, Managing Director at Goldman Sachs, has some helpful tips. Kerr proposes that the first thing to realize is that you are eligible for any reward system you create for yourself. Make the benefits visible: see them, touch them, smell them, hear them, and taste them. For example, see your success in the acquisition of a high-end automobile, touch its leather-wrapped steering wheel, inhale the new-car aroma, hear your new electronics, and celebrate your achievement in a favorite restaurant.[4] Kerr elaborates, "For maximum effectiveness, rewards must also be timely. Aim for prompt recognition since that strengthens the connection between your performance and reward." Also, "Use reversibility if necessary. Take rewards away from yourself if you do not feel that you earned them."[5]

Personal success, however, is at least partially contingent on how early you begin your future orientation. Some fortunate people launch themselves at a very young age, while others have to wait on an opportunity to focus on a lifelong profession. You may climb the corporate ladder only to find that it has been leaning in a wrong direction, and unfortunately you only discover this when you get to the top.[6] Are you climbing the right ladder? If not, can you get off now and still have time to find the right ladder to climb?

Brain Science

Deciphering what motivates us as human beings is a centuries-old puzzle that some of history's most influential thinkers—among them Aristotle, Adam Smith, Sigmund Freud, and Abraham Maslow—have struggled to understand.[7] Such luminaries did not have the advantage of knowledge gleaned from modern brain science. A new model of motivation posits four drives that are hardwired into our brains. These are the drives to acquire, bond, comprehend, and defend.[8]

Arnold Schwarzenegger once said, "What you do is create a vision of who you want to be, and then live into that picture as if it were already true."[9] You are hardwired with drives that stem from your basic instincts, and your belief system is crucial to your success.

Are you ready to accept the challenge of motivation? Can you dedicate the necessary time and effort to plan your future? Is money holding you back from achieving your goals? If you can take money out of the motivational equation, you can enjoy what you already have. Focus on the more important things in life.[10]

Extrinsic Rewards

Carrot-and-stick motivation, also known as extrinsic motivation, is neither adequate nor effective when you are motivating yourself. Here are a few reasons why extrinsic rewards do not motivate: they diminish intrinsic rewards; they are temporary; and they assume that we are driven by lower needs.[11]

How do you feel about rewards? Do you wait for others to motivate you? Find a reason that will inspire you to become more motivated. Then frame it and place it on your refrigerator door or computer screen. Send yourself reminders of the project's deadline by using Outlook or some other means. Become a premier strategist of your own destiny. The reason for doing so is that one person's reward may be another person's punishment.[12] Therefore, you are motivated by rewards that you value most. Once you determine that, motivation will follow naturally.

By understanding your leadership capabilities, you can develop them further. Make sense of things that impact you; build a network of trusting relationships; visualize a compelling image of the future; and invent new ways of doing things.[13]

Are you vulnerable to accepting a promotion that may result in failure? Can you foresee problems with advancing your career too soon? If so, you may experience the "Peter Principle," which entails the idea that promotions may not always lead to greater demonstrations of competence. Advancement up the corporate ladder is often based on factors other than proven merit.[14] Extrinsic rewards are the leading source of motivational impetus for career striving.[15] You therefore must be aware of the fact that movement up the corporate latter may not always be to your benefit. You must become your own career counselor by developing the necessary skills to remain competitive and to prevent the chance of being regarded as incompetent in a new position.

How about your boss? Is she or he toxic to your well-being? Is your boss a jerk? Some 60–75 percent of employees see their immediate supervisors as the "worst and most stressful aspect of their job."[16] One company states that its goal is a "jerk-free" workplace; another declares, "We have a no-jerk rule around here. Hotshots who alienate colleagues are told to change or leave."[17] Seek out leaders who will help you to grow and prosper.

Perhaps you are lucky enough to have a great leader who will help you to achieve personal excellence, but what if you are limiting your own progress? Attempt to identify behaviors that may be holding you back in life, behaviors such as winning at all costs, clinging to the past, and never being able to say you are sorry. If you demonstrate any of these behaviors, you have to refocus and change.[18] One way to refocus is to gather feedback that identifies the specific behaviors you need to alter. Then fix the problem by apologizing for your behavioral flaws, revealing your effort to change, expressing gratitude for others' contributions to your change process, and monitoring your progress.[19]

When you are attempting to reinvent yourself, fragments of motivational theories are not enough and may actually mislead you. Motivation should come from a mix of four things: responsibilities, relationships, rewards, and reasons.[20] Take responsibility for your decisions. When you choose a profession, build supportive relationships and networks. When you land your first job, celebrate your success. Then give yourself reasons to work even harder on advancing in your profession so that you can attain personal excellence.

You are motivated when your *responsibilities* are meaningful and engage your abilities and values. The most motivating tasks are those that stretch you to develop your skills. You are motivated by good *relationships* with colleagues on your path to personal excellence. Appreciation and recognition are the kinds of *rewards* that strengthen relationships, and *reasons* can be the most powerful motivators of all.[21]

Do you sometimes feel that your age may be holding you back? Age-related changes do take place in motivation, and they can be both negative and positive.[22] With increasing age your human capital diminishes.[23] Human capital refers to the stock of knowledge and skills that enable you to perform work and produce economic value.[24] At the start of your career, therefore, you should invest heavily in building up your human capital because toward the end of your career it declines.[25]

Have you built up your human capital? Do you feel slightly burned out in your career? If so, this may be because you become less active as you age. A study of 56 college professors revealed that physically active people process data faster and experience a slower decline in information-processing speed than inactive people as they age.[26]

Life Stages

During your life journey you leave behind a part of yourself and renew yourself at each stage. Do you transition well from one stage of life to another? Knowing the various stages will help to guide you on your path to self-actualization.[27]

The most important stage happens during the first five years of life when you begin to form an intrinsic motivation to learn and grow. Grammar and secondary school then prepared you for your next important experience—college. There you expanded your intellectual horizons and discovered a sense of inner direction. After you graduated, you began your first professional assignment. At this stage you got in, broke in, and began to fit in. Getting in is crucial because, depending on the economic climate at time of graduation, you have to sell yourself and hone your skill set to secure your first job.

Breaking in is usually a fascinating stage. While you may be anxious in your first professional post, you soon discover that the environment is not all about work. It is just as much about shop talk, water-cooler talk, and philosophical talk. The work milieu is not as rigid as you probably thought it would be. Fitting in then becomes a natural process as your skills transfer from the classroom to the office, trade, or business. At this stage you progress upward in Maslow's hierarchy until you reach self-actualization.

Have you reached the life stage at which you are doing what you love? You can reach your full potential by mastering self-motivation and achieving personal excellence. The way to progress through life stages is to deviate from the norm. You become excellent by choosing a path that involves calculated risk and reward. You do this because it brings enormous personal satisfaction, and that is the key to your success in life.[28]

Success in your life is based on your own circumstance. If you are doing what you love and preparing for a rewarding career, then you feel exhilarated and energized. You do this because it is the right thing to do; it puts you in motion, and sets you up for continual improvement. Awake each day happy to be able to contribute to your knowledge and skill level so that you can increase personal excellence. Embrace risk coupled with innovation and creativity so you can master self-motivation. Design a life worth living by creating the things-to-do each day to fulfill your dream. Prioritize the most important things to do each day and make the sacrifice of time and effort now to achieve your goals. Think of yourself as preparing a personal excellence campaign by selecting your friends, mentors, and leaders wisely. Doing so will help you reach personal excellence and make yourself, and everyone else, proud of you.

Reaching and sustaining excellence usually requires internally driven leadership that is highly disciplined and not afraid of risk.[29] Risk was natural for John Gutfreund, the former CEO of Salomon Brothers who exhorted traders to come to work each morning "ready to bite the ass off a bear."[30]

Personal Excellence

Equity theory, Maslow's hierarchy of needs, Expectancy theory, McGregor's theory X and Y, and other motivational models all indicate that people fall into some category of achievement. Plenty of people fall into lower achievement levels, but the possibility of fame and fortune can prompt you to pursue personal excellence.

The one thing that may keep you from rising above your comfort zone and attempting to pick more than low-hanging fruit is the fear of failure. Nothing is a greater deterrent than the fear of failure. Failure, however, is never final. Failure is simply a way of learning the lessons you need to succeed. All great men and women developed the habit of confronting their fear of failure, and acting in spite of their fear, until the habit of courage became part of their character.[31] As Henry Ford said, "Failure is just another opportunity to more intelligently begin again."[32]

Do you look at failure as a possibility, or do you assume that failure is not an option? What constitutes the challenge to achieve for one individual poses the threat of failure for another. The tendency to avoid failure associated with anxiety is as fundamentally important a factor in achievement-oriented action as the tendency to achieve success. No one feels bad when he or she fails at a very difficult task, but to fail when a task appears easy is a source of great embarrassment.[33]

The older you get, the greater the challenges you will face. Great people of the past had many critics, and if they had let those critics hinder their progress, they would not have reached their respective levels of success. If you have a high level of aspiration, perhaps you are destined for far greater things than you once imagined. Aspiration always comes with some degree of anxiety. The price you pay for achievement-oriented action is the experience of anxiety, which is proportionate to the strength of your effort to overcome obstacles to personal excellence.[34]

Have you ever wondered whether motivation is gender specific? More women and minorities are successful today than ever before. How did women in particular break through the proverbial glass ceiling? The reason is that they adopted more competitively assertive tendencies in their fields of professional endeavor.[35]

No matter how you look at motivation, you still have to come to grips with success and failure. Both have two different effects. One is the cognitive-learning effect, which involves a view of change as leading to success. The other is the immediate-motivator effect, which involves the assumption that success has greater reinforcement value than failure.[36]

After you experience initial success in your endeavors, you have a stronger expectation of the same outcome in future projects. Every experience you have is important in cultivating an orientation to repeated successes in life.

Learning is related to motivation as drive, which transforms habit into performance. Drive does not direct, guide, steer, or select particular responses but instead energizes all responses equally. Drive, therefore, multiplies habit to produce the potential for success.[37]

Drive, therefore, is something that you can nurture. Convert knowledge into action by developing plans that specify desired results and constraints. Include checkpoints for how you will spend your time, and revise plans to reflect new opportunities. Take responsibility for decisions by ensuring that each specifies who is accountable for carrying it out, when it must be implemented, and who will be affected. This approach enables you to correct poor decisions. Focus on opportunities, not problems, by getting positive results.[38]

Where can you make the greatest contribution as you learn to develop yourself? How can you stay young and mentally alive during a fifty-year working life? How and when will you change what you do, how you do it, and when you do it?[39] Answering these questions will help you to master self-motivation and prepare you for personal excellence.

By motivating yourself you can become an expert at something you love to do. You thereby will experience a greater sense of pride, accomplishment, and recognition at work and at home.[40]

Lightening Up Your Life

Constructive thought patterns help you to reinvent yourself. Learn to recognize automatic thoughts and make your inner dialogue process-oriented.[41]

Automatic thoughts are hard to control. They can derive from traumatic situations. War veterans, for example, sometimes have recurring thoughts that carry them back to the battlefield. However, you need not have been in battle to experience negative thoughts. When they arise, and they will, focus on your previous successes. This inner dialogue with yourself will begin to run a 30-second commercial in your mind of how successful you are. Remember: you are a winner, so lighten up and focus on WINNING!

Now that you know the art of constructive thinking, set some lifetime goals. Did you ever consider goals that span five to fifteen years out from where you are? Lou Holtz, the former football coach at Notre Dame University, set lifelong goals. He wrote down over 100 goals that he wanted to accomplish in his lifetime, including goals such as wanting all his children to go to college and meeting the President of the United States.[42]

The movie titled *The Bucket List* depicts what happens when you wait too long to achieve your goals. Two terminally ill men escape from a cancer ward and head off on a road trip with a wish list of things to do before they die.[43] Can you create a bucket list? *Now* is the time to prepare that list while you are still young and vibrant.

Summary

Extrinsic rewards are important to all of us, but the carrot-and-stick system gets old quickly. You need to generate new ideas that can help you innovate and create. Extrinsic rewards lead you to focus on them rather than the intrinsic satisfaction you get from accomplishing a challenging task.[44] Concentrate instead on intrinsic motivation, which will help you to reach personal excellence.

By lightening up, remaining positive, and by being happy, you can master self-motivation.

Before we part, I have one more thing for you to consider—something about the Sun's coming up tomorrow.

> *Every morning in Africa, a gazelle wakes up. It knows it must run faster than the fastest lion or it will be killed. Every morning a lion wakes up. It knows it must outrun the slowest gazelle or it will starve to death. It doesn't matter whether you are a lion or a gazelle ... when the Sun comes up, you'd better be running.*[45]

About the Author

Dr. Provitera is an expert in motivation and organizational behavior and provides executive consulting to small business owners, managers, and leaders. He is an Associate Professor at Barry University in Miami (Florida), where he teaches organizational behavior at both the undergraduate and graduate level. He has 15 years of Wall Street executive experience at various investment banks such as Merrill Lynch, Morgan Stanley, and Solomon Brothers. In his last position at Mizuho Financial Group, he was an Assistant Vice President of Fixed Income Operations where he managed 14 people.

Dr. Provitera has authored and coauthored a number of presentations and papers in a variety of national (i.e., Montreal Canada, Texas, California, Chicago, Cincinnati, Denver, Fort Lauderdale, Hawaii, Miami, New Jersey, New York, Orlando, Philadelphia, Seattle, Boston, and Washington, DC) forums and outlets, as well as publications in the *Academic Exchange Quarterly*, the *Academy of Management Executive*, the *Encyclopedia of Human Resources Information Systems*, the *Journal of Applied Management and Entrepreneurship*, the *Journal of Business and Economic Research*, the *Journal of College Teaching and Learning*, the *Journal of Management Education*, the *Management Case Study Journal*, and the *Marketing Management Journal*. Moreover and to his credit, he has complemented these presentations and papers with extensive professional development activities and service, including serving as an editorial board member and peer reviewer, conference session chair, textbook reviewer, and article referee for the *Academy of Management*, the *International Journal of Management*, and the *Southwest Academy of Management*.

Dr. Provitera is very active at the Academy of Management annual meetings. He has presented various research, facilitated and cochaired doctoral professional development workshops, and created and attended several professional development workshops. He is also a certified leadership trainer for Situational Leadership from the Center for Leadership Studies, Escondido, California. He was trained by Dr. Paul Hersey, who is a behaviorist and a well-known management trainer.

Dr. Provitera volunteers his time to the Kids and The Power of Work Program (KAPOW) at elementary schools in Miami, Florida. In this capacity, he teaches business skills to fourth graders.

Dr. Provitera serves as a subject specialist for the Distance Education and Training Council (DETC) as site evaluator, graduate and undergraduate course evaluator, and overall program evaluation. The DETC is a global leader in distance learning accreditation.

He can be contacted regarding his seminars, management training, and keynote speaking engagements at docprov@msn.com or visit his website at http://docprov.com.

Notes

Chapter 1

1. Fayol and Gray (1984).
2. Deci and Ryan (2001).
3. Ditto.
4. Koestner, Ryan, Bernieri, and Hold (1984).
5. Ryan and Connell (1989).
6. Ryan (1982).
7. Livingston (1971).
8. Lencioni (2009).
9. Jones and Jones (2009).
10. Dewhurst (2009).
11. Rohn (2011).
12. Waitley (2010).
13. Kerr (2008).
14. Krzyzewski (2006).
15. Ancona, Malone, Orlikowski, and Senge (2007).
16. Goffee and Jones (2000).
17. Jack (1932).
18. Deci and Ryan (2001).

Chapter 2

1. Vroom (1964).
2. Franken (2002).
3. Romando (2010).
4. Jones and George (2009).
5. Dunham (2004).
6. LePine, LePine, and Jackson (2004).
7. Baptiste (1800).
8. Pinchot (1985).
9. Provitera (2011).
10. George, Sims, McLean, and Mayer (2007).
11. George (2006).
12. Drucker (1993).
13. Drucker (2005).

14. Ditto.
15. Sedgwick (1888).
16. Brewer and Hewstone (2004).
17. Grown Up (movie) (2011).
18. Robbins (2011).
19. Courageous (movie) (2011).
20. Gottfried (2007).
21. The Geisha Boy (movie) (1958).
22. Woody Allen (2011).
23. Miracle (movie) (2004).
24. Bonabeau and Meyer (2001).
25. Butler (2008).
26. Lavoie (2007).
27. Antonakis and House (2002).
28. Javitch (2009).
29. Herzberg (2003).
30. Lavoie (2007).
31. Pounds (2006).
32. Ditto.
33. SWOT analysis (2011).
34. Weiner, Russell, and Lerman (1978).
35. Lawler (1994).
36. Cartwright (2008).
37. Dweck (1990).
38. Dweck and Leggett (1988).
39. Ditto.
40. Ditto.
41. Ditto.
42. Ditto.
43. Lavoie (2007).
44. Ditto.
45. The Godfather (movie) (2011).
46. Dyer (1992).
47. Rohn (2010).
48. Jobs (2005).
49. Welch (2011).
50. Kenji (2011).
51. Hill (2011).
52. Rohn (2010).
53. Vroom (1964).
54. Hellriegal and Slocum (2011).

55. Raico (2010).
56. Lawler and Suttle (1972).
57. Boring (1950); Allport (1954).
58. Provitera-McGlynn (2001).

Chapter 3

1. Coffin (2011).
2. Winnie the Pooh, Walt Disney Corporation (2011).
3. Dyer (1992).
4. Cavalier (2000).
5. Maslow (2010).
6. Maslow (1943).
7. Ditto.
8. Hall and Nougaim (1968); Lawler and Suttle (1972).
9. Pierce and Bell (2011).
10. Cullen, White, Pierce, and Usher (2000).
11. Lewin (1935).
12. Alderfer (1977).
13. Ditto.
14. Maslow, Maslow, and Gieger (1993).

Chapter 4

1. Neck and Manz (2007), p. 5.
2. Ditto.
3. Drucker (2005).
4. Chandler (1996).
5. Gilkey and Kilts (2007).
6. Schwarz and McCarthy (2007).
7. Hallowell (2005).
8. Lowe (2009).
9. Illeris (2011).
10. Ditto.
11. Victor Vroom (2011).
12. Vroom (1964).
13. Ditto.
14. Porter and Lawler (2011).
15. Porter and Lawler (1968).
16. Quick (1980).
17. Clawson (2008).

18. Castelli (2008).
19. Gardner (2009).
20. Ditto.
21. Robins (1992).
22. Energizer (2010).
23. Wright (2010).
24. Cottrell (2009).
25. Landro (2010).
26. Daly (1982).
27. Seligman (1998).
28. Seligman (2004); Gardner (2009).
29. Fayol (2011).
30. Brunsson (2008).
31. Wren and Bedeian (2009).
32. Pajares (2002).
33. Bandura (1997); Bandura (1976); Bandura and Dweck (1985).

Chapter 5

1. Gupta and Shaw (1998).
2. Deci and Ryan (1994).
3. Thomas (2000), p. 6.
4. Deci and Ryan (1991), pp. 237–288.
5. Deci and Ryan (2001).
6. Csikszentmihalyi (1998).
7. Murray (1938); Goldstein (1939).
8. Deci and Ryan (2001).
9. Herzberg (1987); Feder (2000); Herzberg (1959).
10. Gray (2004).
11. Herzberg (1987).
12. Herzberg (1959).
13. Nightingale (2010).
14. Heifetz and Laurie (2001).
15. Fairholm (1996).
16. Quinn (1996).
17. Shelp (1984).
18. Luthans, Youssef, and Avolio (2007).
19. Quinn (1996), p. 36.
20. Quinn (1996), p. 35.
21. Simon (1955); Simon (1957); Simon (1981).
22. Goleman (2004).

23. Etzioni (1988).
24. Thomas (2000).
25. Thomas and Velthouse (1990).
26. Thomas (2000); Csikszentmihalyi (1998).
27. Thomas and Tymon (1993).
28. Ditto.
29. Herzberg, Mausner, and Snyderman (1959).

Chapter 6

1. Great Oaks Proverb (2011).
2. Cook (2009).
3. Clawson (2008).
4. Locus of Control (2011).
5. The Scorpion and the Frog (2011).
6. Bipp (2009).
7. Barrick, Mount, and Judge (2001).
8. Judge, Heller, and Mount (2002).
9. Bipp (2009).
10. Burns (1978).
11. Thomas and Velthouse (1990).
12. Ellis (2005).
13. White (2003).
14. Kapnis (2007).
15. McCormick (2000).
16. Fiske (2008).
17. Maltz (1989).
18. GlaxoSmithKline (2009).
19. Maltz (1989).
20. Martin (2011).
21. Holt (1989), p. 230.
22. Fiske (1989), p. 253, 283.
23. Aristotle (2011).
24. Dunham (2004).
25. Soegaard (2011).
26. Kunda (1999); Simon (1957; 1981), as cited in Kunda 1999.
27. Kerr (1995).
28. Blau and Scott (1962).
29. Kerr (1995).
30. Dunham (2004).
31. Robbins and Judge (2011).

32. Cross (1999), p. 21.
33. Bash (2003), p. 213.
34. Cary (1641).
35. Felder and Solomon (2010).
36. Ralph Waldo Emerson quote (2011).
37. Neck and Manz (2007), p. 5.
38. McGregor (2011).
39. Ditto.
40. Waterman (1994), p. 38.
41. Ditto.
42. Boleman and Deal (2003), p. 113.
43. Waterman (1994), p. 41.
44. Maslow (2010).
45. Mayo (1933).
46. Herzberg, Mausner, and Snyderman (1959), p. 8.
47. Herzberg, Mausner, and Snyderman (1959), p. 126.
48. Mayo (1933).
49. Newstrom (2002), p. 53.
50. Covey (1990); Covey (1989).
51. Nightingale (2010).
52. Ditto.
53. Couric (2009).
54. Think and Grow Rich (2011).
55. Tracy (2010).
56. Tracy (1993), p. 123.
57. Tracy (1993), p. 123; Tracy (2010); Tracy (2010).
58. Simon and Shuster Audio (1980).
59. Waitley (2010).
60. Ditto.

Chapter 7

1. Andrews (2010).
2. Self Efficacy Site (2011).
3. Brainy Quote (2011).
4. Ditto.
5. Feuer (1974).
6. Andrews (2008); Andrews (2009).
7. Bargh and Chartrand (1999), p. 462.
8. Latona (2009), p. 1.
9. Ditto.

10. Avolio and Luthans (2006).
11. Luthans, Youssef, and Avolio (2007).
12. Luthans (2002).
13. Luthans and Avolio (2007).
14. Ditto.
15. Blanchard (2010).
16. Avolio and Luthans (2006); Sutcliffe and Vogus (2003).
17. Covey (1989); Johnson (2011).
18. Luthans, Youssef, and Avolio (2007).
19. Ditto.
20. Henry David Thoreau quotes.
21. Peters (2010).
22. Blanchard (2011).
23. Luthans, Youssef, and Avolio (2007).
24. Bandura (1976).
25. Four Leaf Clovers (2011).
26. Andrews and Chamberlain (2011).
27. Sificus (2010).
28. Welch and Welch (2005), p. 6.
29. Robbins and Judge (2011).
30. Kolbe (2011).
31. Chapman (2010).
32. The Joneses (movie) (2011).
33. Robins (1992), p. 24.
34. Eastwood (2011).
35. Anand, Glick, and Manz (2002).

Chapter 8

1. Hodgson and White (2001).
2. Atkinson (1965).
3. Lawler (1994).
4. Lowe (2009).
5. Kolbe A Index.
6. Hellriegal and Slocum (2011).
7. Ditto.
8. Neck and Manz (2007).
9. Patterns (movie) (2011).
10. Buscaglia (2012).
11. Zigler (2010).
12. Neural Pathways (2011).

13. Port (2011).
14. Johnson (1927).
15. Simpson (2000).
16. Lewin (1947).
17. Lewin (2012).
18. Cummings and Worley (2009).
19. Kotter (2007).
20. Kotter (2007).
21. Deming (2000).
22. Lewin (2012).
23. Kotter (2007).
24. The Calf's Path by Sam Walter Foss (2011).
25. *The Calf Path*, Sam Walter Foss, written in the late 1800s (1997).

Chapter 9

1. Peck (2003).
2. Butler (2007).
3. Ditto.
4. Kerr (2008).
5. Ditto.
6. Covey (2006).
7. Nohria, Groysberg, and Lee (2008).
8. Nohria, Groysberg, and Lee (2008).
9. Chandler (2004).
10. Kohn (1998).
11. Daft (2008).
12. Clawson (2008).
13. Ancona, Malone, Orlikowski, and Senge (2007).
14. Peter and Hull (1969); Hull (1931).
15. Raynor (1978).
16. Domurad (2010).
17. Ditto.
18. Goldsmith and Reiter (2007).
19. Ditto.
20. Maccoby (2010).
21. Ditto.
22. Stroebe (2010).
23. Diamond (1984).
24. Stroebe (2010).
25. Diamond (1984).

26. Neck and Manz (2007).
27. Dowler (2010).
28. Quinn (1996).
29. Quinn (1996).
30. John Gutfruend quote (2011).
31. Akrura-Gita Coaching (2010).
32. Henry Ford quote (2011).
33. Atkinson and Birch (1970).
34. Atkinson (1965).
35. Mead (1949).
36. Atkinson and Birch (1970).
37. Beck (2004).
38. Drucker (2005).
39. Drucker (1999).
40. Harvard Business School Publishing (2006).
41. Franken (2002).
42. Holtz (1999).
43. *The Bucket List* (movie) (2011).
44. McClelland (1985).
45. Found on website http://thinkexist.com/quotation/every_morning_in_africa-a_gazelle_wakes_up-it/298139.html on September 18, 2011.

References

Akrura-Gita Coaching: Ideas and tools for your spiritual and professional success (2010). *Failure is a great teacher*. Retrieved October 17, 2011, from http://gitacoaching.blogspot.com/2010/03/failure-is-great-teacher.html

Alderfer, C. P. (1977). Improving organizational communication through long-term intergroup intervention. *Journal of Applied Behavioral Science 13*, 193–210.

Allport, G. W. (1954). *The nature of prejudice*. Reading, MA: Addison Wesley.

Anand, V., Glick, W. H., & Manz, C. C. (2002). Thriving on the knowledge of outsiders: Tapping organizational social capital. *Academy of Management Executive 16*(1), 87–101.

Ancona, D., Malone, T. W., Orlikowski, W. J., & Senge, P. M. (2007). In praise of the incomplete leader. *Harvard Business Review*.

Andrews, A., & Chamberlain, J. (2011). Retrieved September 17, 2011, from http://www.youtube.com/watch?v=T3XagavMnxM

Andrews, A. (2008). *The butterfly effect*. Retrieved October 11, 2010, from http://www.youtube.com/watch?v=FnwddVuhW8c

Andrews, A. (2009). *The butterfly effect*. Retrieved October 6, 2010, from http://www.youtube.com/watch?v=-PggnK1FC3o

Andrews, A. (2010). *The boy who changed the world*. Nashville, TN: Tommy Nelson Publishers.

Antonakis, J., & House, R. (2002). An analysis of the full-range leadership theory: The way forward. In *Transformational and Charismatic Leadership: The Road Ahead* (pp. 3–35). The Netherlands: Elsevier.

Aristotle (2011). Retrieved September 24, 2011, from http://classics.mit.edu/Aristotle/physics.2.ii.html

Atkinson, J. W. (1965). The mainsprings of achievement-oriented activity. In J. W. Atkinson & J. O. Raynor (Eds.), *Personality, motivation, and achievement*. New York: John Wiley & Sons.

Atkinson, J. W., & Birch, D. (1970). The dynamics of achievement-oriented activity. In J. W. Atkinson & J. O. Raynor (Eds.), *Personality, motivation, and achievement*. New York: John Wiley & Sons.

Avolio, B. J., & Luthans, F. (2006). *The high impact leader: Moments matter in accelerating authentic leadership development*. New York: McGraw-Hill.

Bandura, A. (1976). *Social learning theory*. Englewood Cliffs, NJ: Prentice-Hall.

Bandura, A. (1997). *Self-efficacy: The exercise of control*. New York: W. H. Freeman and Company.

Bandura, M. M., & Dweck, C. S. (1985). *The relationship of conceptions on intelligence and achievement goals to achievement-related cognition, affect and behavior.* Harvard University (Unpublished manuscript).

Bargh, J. A., & Chartrand, T. L. (1999). The unbearable automaticity of being. *American Psychologist 54,* 462–479.

Barrick, M. R., Mount, M. K., & Judge, T. A. (2001). Personality and performance at the beginning of the new millennium: What do we know and where do we go next? *International Journal of Selection and Assessment 9,* 9–30.

Bash, L. (2003). *Adult learners in the academy.* Bolton, MA: Anker Publishing Company Inc, p. 213.

Beck, R. C. (2004). *Motivation: Theories and principles* (5th ed.). Upper Saddle River, NJ: Pearson Education Inc., p. 153.

Bipp, T. (2009). Linking personality to work motivation and performance: Individual difference effects. In M. Wosnitza, S. A. Karabenick, A. Efklides, & P. Nenniger (Eds.), *Contemporary motivation research: From global to local perspectives.* Hogrefe Publishing.

Blanchard, K. (2010). *Meet the masterminds: Ken Blanchard on the one minute entrepreneur. Interview by* Michael W. McLaughlin, *Management Consulting News. Retrieved October 20, 2010, from* http://www.managementconsultingnews.com/interviews/blanchard_interview.php

Blanchard, K. (2011). Retrieved September 24, 2011, from http://www.kenblanchard.com/Store/Books_Audios/The_One_Minute_Manager_Essentials/One_Minute_Manager_The/

Blau, P. M., & Scott, W. R. (1962). *Formal organizations: A comparative approach.* San Francisco, CA: Chandler Publishing Company.

Boleman, L. G., & Deal, T. E. (2003). *Reframing organizations: Artistry, choice, and Leadership* (3rd ed.). Jossey Bass Publishers, p. 113.

Bonabeau, E., & Meyer, C. Swarm intelligence: A whole new way to think about business. *Harvard Business Review.*

Boring, E. G. (1950). *A history of experimental psychology.* Englewood Cliffs, NJ: Prentice-Hall.

Brainy quote (2011). *Thomas Edison.* Retrieved August 4, 2011, from http://www.brainyquote.com/quotes/authors/t/thomas_a_edison.html

Brewer, M. B., & Hewstone, M. (2004). *Emotion and motivation.* New York: Blackwell Publishing.

Brunsson, K. (2008). Some effects of fayolism. *International Studies of Management and Organization 38*(1), 30.

Burns, J. M. (1978). *Leadership.* New York: Harper and Row Publishers.

Buscaglia, L. (2012). *Famous quotes.* Retrieved September 11, 2011, from http://thinkexist.com/quotation/worry_never_robs_tomorrow_of_its_sorrow-it_only/213606.html

Butler, T. (2007). Moving from impasse to action: How to decide which path to take. *Harvard Business Review*. (Excerpted from *Getting unstuck: How dead ends become new paths*.)

Butler, T. (2008). Learning to let our passions guide us. In Getting unstuck: How dead end jobs become new paths. *Harvard Business Review*.

Cartwright, T. (2008). The leadership value of setting priorities. *Leadership in Action*. San Francisco, CA, 27(6), 18.

Cary, L. (1641). *It is not necessary to change, it is necessary not to change*. Lucious Cary, 2nd Viscount Falkland in a speech in the House of Commons on 1641-11-22. Retrieved September 28, 2010, from http://en.wikiquote.org/wiki/Edmund_Burke

Castelli, P. A. (2008). The leader as motivator: Coach and self-esteem builder. *Management Research News 31*(10), 717–728.

Cavalier, R. P. (2000). *Personal motivation: A model for decision making*. Westport, CT: Praeger Publishers.

Chandler, S. (1996). *100 Ways to motivate yourself*. Career Press Inc.

Chandler, S. (2004). *100 Ways to motivate yourself: Change your life forever*. Career Press Publishers.

Chapman, A. (2010). *Adam's equity theory: J. Stacy Adams, equity theory on job motivation*. Retrieved October 12, 2010, from http://www.businessballs.com/adamsequitytheory.htm

Clawson, J. G. (2008). *Level three leadership: Getting below the surface* (4th ed.). Englewood Cliffs, NJ: Prentice Hall.

Coffin, W. S. (2011). *Even if you win the rat race, you're still a rat*. Retrieved September 13, 2011, from http://en.wikipedia.org/wiki/William_Sloane_Coffin

Cook, S. E. (2009). *Eliminating negative thoughts: 3 Ways to usher in the positive*. Retrieved June 9, 2011, from http://EzineArticles.com/2046214

Cottrell, D. (2009). *Monday morning motivation: Five steps that will energize your team, customers, and profits*. Harper Business, p. 150.

Courageous (2011). Retrieved October 14, 2011, from http://www.courageousthemovie.com/themovie

Couric, K. (2009). *Sullenberger recalls the moment that the engines died: Katie Couric interviews the amazing pilot and crew of US Airways Flight 1549*. Retrieved September 21, 2010, from http://www.cbsnews.com/stories/2009/01/30/60minutes/main4764852.shtml

Covey, S. R. (1989). *The seven habits of highly effective people: Powerful lessons in personal change*. New York: Simon & Schuster.

Covey, S. R. (1990). *Principled-centered leadership*. New York: Simon & Schuster.

Covey, S. R. (2006). *The 8th habit: From effectiveness to greatness*. Running Press Miniature Editions.

Cross, K. P. (1999). *Learning is about making connections. League for innovation for community colleges.* Mission Viejo, CA, p. 21.

Csikszentmihalyi, M. (1998). *Finding flow: The psychology of engagement in everyday life.* New York: Basic Books.

Cullen, D., White, R. E., Pierce, B., & Usher, J. M. (2000). DIALOGUE. *Academy of Management Review 25*(4), 696–701.

Cummings, T. G., & Worley, C. G. (2009). *Organizational development and change.* Southwest Learning.

Daft, R. L. (2008). *The leadership experience.* Thompson South-Western, p. 239

Daly, J. (1982). *Stronger: Trading brokenness for incredible strength.* Thomas Nelson Inc.

Deci, E. L., & Ryan, R. M. (1994). Promoting self determined education. *Scandinavian Journal of Educational Research 38*, 3–41.

Deci, E. L., & Ryan, R. M. (2001). A motivational approach to self: Integration in personality. In *Nebraska Symposium on Motivation* 1990: Perspectives on Motivation. Current Theory and Research in Motivation, R. A. Dienstbier (Ed.), Vol. 38, pp. 237–288, Lincoln, NE.

Deming, W. E. (2000). *Out of crisis.* The MIT Press.

Dewhurst, S. (2009). How to regain your motivation for work. *Strategic Communication Management, 13*(3), 14.

Diamond, A. M. (1984). An economic model of the life-cycle research productivity of scientists. *Scientometrics 6*, 189–196.

Domurad, F. (2010). The managerial trap: Sometimes getting rid of bad leaders is more important than finding great ones. *CorrectionsOne News.* Retrieved March 4, 2010, from http://www.correctionsone.com/jail-management/articles/3083607-The-managerial-trap/

Dowler, C. A. (2010). *The eight stages of life.* ManifestYourPotential.com. Retrieved November 8, 2010, from http://www.manifestyourpotential.com/life/make_sense_of_life/life_stages/topic_eight_life_stages.htm

Drucker, P. F. (1993). *The practice of management.* Collins Publishers.

Drucker, P. F. (1999). *Management challenges for the 21st century.* Harper Collins Publishers, p. 63.

Drucker, P. F. (2005). Managing oneself. *Harvard Business Review.*

Drucker, P. F. (2005). What makes an effective executive? *Harvard Business Review.*

Dunham, R. (2004). *The manager's workshop.* Englewood Cliffs, NJ: Prentice-Hall Publishers.

Dweck, C. S. (1990). Self-theories and goals: Their role in motivation, personality, and development. In *Nebraska Symposium on Motivation* 1990: Perspectives on Motivation. Current Theory and Research in Motivation, R. A. Dienstbier (Ed.).

Dweck, C. S., & Leggett. E. L. (1988). A social-cognitive approach to personality and motivation. *Psychological Review 95*, 256–273.

Dyer, W. (1992). *Real magic: Creating miracles in everyday life*. New York: Harper Collins Publishers.

Eastwood, C. (2011). *Magnum force*. Retrieved September 17, 2011, from http://www.imdb.com/find?s=all&q=magnum+force

Ellis, J. J. (2005). *His Excellency: George Washington*. New York: Random House Publishers.

Energizer (2010). Retrieved September 14, 2010, from http://www.energizer.com/energizer-bunny/Pages/bunny-history.aspxo

Etzioni, A. (1988). *The moral dimension: Toward a new economics*. New York: Free Press.

Fairholm, G. (1996). Spiritual leadership: Fulfilling whole-self needs at work. *Leadership and Organizational Development Journal, 17*(5), 11–17.

Fayol, H. (2011). Retrieved September 15, 2011, from http://www.managers-net.com/Biography/Fayol.html

Fayol, H., & Gray, I. (1984). *General and Industrial Management*. Institute of Electrical and Electronics Engineering.

Feder, B. J. (2000). *F. I. Herzberg, 76, Professor and management consultant*. New York Times, February 1, 2000, C26.

Felder, R. M., & Solomon, B. A. (2010). *Index of learning styles questionnaire*. Retrieved October 4, 2010, from http://www.ncsu.edu/felder-public/RMF.html

Feuer, L. S. (1974). *Einstein and the generations of science*. New York: Basic Books

Fiske, S. T. (1989). Examining the role of intent: Toward understanding its role in stereotyping and prejudice. In J. Uleman & J. Bargh (Eds.), *Unintended thought: The limits of awareness, intention, and control*. New York: Guilford Press, pp. 253–283.

Fiske, S. T. (2008). Core social motivations: Views from the couch, consciousness, classroom, computers, and collectives. In J. Y. Shah & W. L. Gardner (Eds.), *Handbook of Motivation Science*. New York: Guilford Publications Inc.

Four Leaf Clovers (2011). Retrieved September 17, 2011, from http://www.fourleafclover.com/vshop/facts_about_4-leaf_clovers.html

Franken, R. E. (2002). *Human motivation* (5th ed.). Belmont, CA: Wadsworth/Thomson Learning.

Gardner, C. (2009). *Start where you are: Life lessons on getting where you are to where you want to be*. New York: Harper Collins Publishing.

Gardner, C. (2009). 'Happyness' author Gardner hopes we are each our own champ. *Marin Independent Journal*. Retrieved from http://www.chrisgardnermedia.com/images/press_clippings/Marin_Independent_Journal_090513.pdf

George, B. (2006). Truly authentic leadership. *U.S. News & World Report, 141*(16), 52–54.

George, W., Sims, P., McLean A., & Mayer, D. (2007). Discovering your authentic leadership. *Harvard Business Review, 85*(2), 129–138.

Gilkey, R., & Kilts, C. (2007). Cognitive fitness. *Harvard Business Review*.

GlaxoSmithKline (2009). Retrieved July 19, 2011, from http://www.gumsmart.co.uk/campaign/habit.shtml.

Goffee, R., & Jones, G. (2000). Why should anyone be led by you? *Harvard Business Review*.

Goldsmith, M., & Reiter, M. (2007). *What got you here won't get you there.* Hyperion Books.

Goldstein, K. (1939). *The organism.* New York: American Book Co.

Goleman, D. (2004). What makes a leader? *Harvard Business Review.*

Gottfried, M. (2007). *Coach's challenge: Faith, football, and filling the father gap.* New York: Simon & Shuster.

Gray, L. (2004). Rethinking money and motivation. *Harvard Business Review.*

Great Oaks Proverb (2011). Retrieved October 13, 2011, from http://www.baudville.com/recognition-themes/Dedication/Growing-with-Each-Day/rs/3/88/award-trophies

Grown Up (movie) (2011). Retrieved September 14, 2011, from http://www.imdb.com/title/tt1375670/

Gupta, N., & Shaw, J. D. (1998). Let the evidence speak: Financial rewards are effective!" *Compensation and Benefits Review*, 26–32.

Hall, D. T., & Nougaim, K. E. (1968). An examination of Maslow's need hierarchy in and organizational setting. *Organizational Behavior and Human Performance 3*, 12–35.

Hallowell, E. M. (2005). Overloaded circuits: Why smart people underperform. *Harvard Business Review.*

Harvard Business School Publishing (2006). *Motivation: The not-so-secret ingredient of high performance. Excerpted from performance management: Measure and improve the effectiveness of your employees.* Boston, MA: Harvard Business School Press.

Heifetz, R. A., & Laurie, D. L. (2001). The work of leadership. *Harvard Business Review.*

Hellriegal, D., & Slocum, J. W. (2011). *Organizational behavior* (13th ed.). Cengage Learning.

Henry David Thoreau quotes. *Retrieved September 16, 2011, from* http://www.angelfire.com/ma4/memajs/quotes/life.html

Henry Ford quote (2011). Retrieved September 17, 2011, from http://gitacoaching.blogspot.com/2010/03/failure-is-great-teacher.html

Herzberg, F. (1959). *The motivation to work*, New York: John Wiley & Sons.

Herzberg, F. (2003). One more time: How do you motivate employees? *Harvard Business Review*.

Herzberg, F. I. (1987). One more time: How do you motivate employees? *Harvard Business Review*, September/October 87, 65(5), 109–120.

Herzberg, F., Mausner, B., & Snyderman, B. B. (1959). *The motivation to work*. New York: John Wiley & Sons.

Hill, N. (2011). *Self success Guru Napolean Hill says*. Retrieved March 31, 2011, from http://www.thebestsuccessguru.com/self-success-guru-napoleon-hill-says.html

Hodgson, P., & White, R. P. (2001). *Relax its only uncertainty: Lead the way when the way is changing*. Prentice Hall Publications.

Holt, R. R. (1989). *Freud reappraised: A fresh look at psychoanalytical theory*. Guilford Publications, Inc, p. 230.

Holtz, L. (1999). *Winning every day: The game plan for success*. Harper Paperbacks.

Hull, C. L. (1931). Goal attraction and directing ideas conceived as habit phenomena. *Psychological Review 38*, 486–506.

Illeris, K. (2011). Workplace and learning. In M. Malloch, L. Cairns, K. Evans,& B. N. O'Connor (Eds.), *The Sage handbook of workplace learning*. Sage Publications.

Jack, L. P. (1932). Retrieved September 13, 2011, from http://en.wikiquote.org/wiki/L._P._Jacks

Javitch, D. (2009, June 19). 5 Employee motivation myths debunked: Recognition, not money, is the real motivator in a down economy. *Employee Management*.

Jobs, S. (2005). *You have to find what you love, Jobs says*. Retrieved September 15, 2011 from http://news.stanford.edu/news/2005/june15/jobs-061505.html

John Gutfruend quote (2011). Retrieved September 17, 2011, from http://www.time.com/time/magazine/article/0,9171,973710,00.html

Johnson, M. (1927). *More maxims of mark*. Retrieved October 17, 2010, from http://en.wikiquote.org/wiki/Mark_Twain

Johnson, S. (2011). *Who moved my cheese*. Retrieved September 16, 2011, from http://www.whomovedmycheese.com/?gclid=CJXxxsqZo6sCFY1S7Aodfm-02g

Jones, G. R., & George, J. M. (2009). *Contemporary management* (6th ed.). New York: McGraw-Hill Publishers.

Judge, T. A., Heller, D., & Mount, M. K. (2002). Five-factor model of personality and job satisfaction: A meta analysis. *Journal of Applied Psychology 87*, 530–541.

Kapnis, L. (2007). *Poor Richard's almanac*. Retrieved September 22, 2010, from http://gse.uml.edu/rtah/pdf/BenFranklin.pdf

Kenji (2011). *Forget your weaknesses. Develop your strengths*. Retrieved March 31, 2011, from http://www.unreadyandwilling.com/2010/01/develop-your-strengths/#comment-849.

Kerr, S. (1995). On the folly of rewarding A while hoping for B. *Academy of Management Executive 9*(1), 7.

Kerr, S. (2008). *Reward systems: Does yours measure up?* Harvard Business Publishing, p. 4.

Koestner, R., Ryan, R. M., Bernieri, F., & Hold, K. (1984). Setting limits on children's behavior: The differential effects of controlling versus informational styles on intrinsic motivation and creativity. *Journal of Personality 52*, 233–248.

Kohn, A. (1998). Challenging behaviorist dogma: Myths about money and motivation (March/April). *Compensation and Benefits Review*.

Kolbe, K. (2011). *Kolbe A Index*. Retrieved August 19, 2011, from http://www.kolbe.com/home.cfm

Kotter, J. P. (2007). Leading change: Why transformation efforts fail. *Harvard Business Review*.

Krzyzewski, M. (2006). *Beyond basketball: Coach K's keywords for success*. Warner Business Books.

Landro, L. (2010). The hidden benefits of exercise: Even moderate physical activity can boost the immune system and protect against chronic diseases. *Wall Street Journal*. The Informed Patient Section, Retrieved January 5, 2010.

Latona, P. (2009). *The butterfly effect: An analogy from quantum physics. The national ledger*. Retrieved October 7, 2010, from http://www.nationalledger.com/cgi-bin/artman/exec/view.cgi?archive=39&num=27093, p. 1.

Lavoie, R. (2007). *The motivational breakthrough: Secrets to turning on the tuned-out-child*. Retrieved from http://www.pbs.org/aboutpbs/news/20071211_richardlavoie.html

Lavoie, R. D. (2007). *The motivational breakthrough: 6 Secrets for turning on the tuned out child*. New York: Touchstone, Simon & Shuster.

Lawler, E. E. III, & Suttle, J. L. (1972). A causal correlation test of the need hierarchy concept. *Organizational Behavior and Human Performance 7*, 265–287.

Lawler, E. E. III. (1994). *Motivation in work organizations*. San Francisco, CA: Jossey-Bass Publishers.

Lencioni, P. (2009). The no-cost way to motivate. *Businessweek*, September edition.

LePine, J. A., LePine, M. A., & Jackson, C. L. (2004). Challenge and hindrance stress: Relationships with exhaustion, motivation to learn and learning performance. *Journal of Applied Psychology 98*, 883–891.

Lewin, K. (1935). *A dynamic theory of personality*. New York: McGraw-Hill Publishers.

Lewin, K. (1947). Frontiers of group dynamics. *Human Relations, 1*, 5–41.

Lewin, K. (2012). *Group decision and social change.* Retrieved August 27, 2011, from http://www.crossroad.to/Quotes/brainwashing/kurt-lewin-change.htm

Livingston, J. S. (1971). Myth of the well educated manager. *Harvard Business Review.*

Locus of Control. Retrieved July 12, 2011, from http://medical-dictionary.thefreedictionary.com/locus+of+control

Lowe, T. (2009). *Get motivated.* Crown Business Publishers.

Luthans, F. (2002). The need for and meaning of positive organizational behavior. *Journal of Organizational Behavior 23,* 695–706.

Luthans, F., & Avolio, B. J. (2007). Positive psychological capital: Measurement and relationship with performance and satisfaction. *Personnel Psychology 60,* 541–572.

Luthans, F., Youssef, C. M., & Avolio, B. J. (2007). *Psychological capital: Developing the human competitive edge.* Oxford: Oxford University Press.

Maccoby, M. (2010). The 4 Rs of motivation. *Research Technology Management 53*(4), 60–61.

Maltz, M. (1989). *Psycho-cybernetics, a new way to get more living out of life.* Pocket Books.

Martin, C. (2011). What is the reticular activating system? Retrieved July 25, 2011, from http://www.wisegeek.com/what-is-the-reticular-activating-system.htm

Maslow, A. H. (1943). A theory of human motivation. *Psychological Review 50,* 370–396.

Maslow, A. H. (2010). *Maslow on management.* Retrieved November 15, 2010, from http://www.altfeldinc.com/pdfs/maslow.pdf

Maslow, A., Maslow, B., & Gieger (1993). *The farther reaches of human nature.* Penguin Arkana Publishing.

Mayo, E. (1933). *The human problems of an industrial civilization.* New York: Macmillan.

McClelland, D. C. (1985). *Human motivation.* Glenview, IL: Scott Foresman.

McCormick, B. (2000). *Ben Franklin's 12 rules of management.* Entrepreneur Press.

McGlynn, A. P. (2001). *Successful beginnings for college teaching: Engaging your students from the first day.* Atwood Publishing.

McGregor, D. (2011). Retrieved September 16, 2011, from http://en.wikipedia.org/wiki/Douglas_McGregor

Mead, M. (1949). *Male and female.* New York: Morrow Publishers.

Miracle (movie) (2004). Retrieved February 25, 2011, from http://www.imdb.com/title/tt0349825/

Murray, H. A. (1938). *Exploitations in personality: A clinical and experimental study of fifty men of collage age.* New York: Oxford University Press

Neck, C. P., & Manz, C. C. (2007). *Mastering self-leadership: Empowering yourself for personal excellence* (4th ed.). Pearson Prentice Hall.

Neural Pathways (2011). Retrieved September 25, 2011, from http://www.reference.md/files/D009/mD009434.html

Newstrom, J. W. (2002). In search of excellence: Its importance and effects. *Academy of Management Executive 16*(1), 53–56.

Nightingale, E. (2010). *Brief excerpt from the strangest secret.* Retrieved September 21, 2010, from http://www.thestrangestsecretmovie.com/

Nohria, N., Groysberg, & Lee, L (2008). Employee motivation: A powerful new model. *Harvard Business Review.*

Pajares, F. (2002). *Overview of social cognitive theory and of self-efficacy.* Retrieved from http://www.emory.edu/EDUCATION/mfp/eff.html

Patterns (movie) (2011). Retrieved September 17, 2011, from http://www.imdb.com/title/tt0049601/

Peck, M. S. (2003). *The road less traveled, 25th Anniversary Edition: A new psychology of love, traditional values and spiritual growth.* Touchstone Publishers.

Peter, L. J., & Hull, R. (1969). *The Peter principle.* New York: Morrow Publishers.

Peters, T. (2010). *The little big things: 163 Ways to pursue excellence.* Harper Business.

Pierce, B. (2011). Recommendations for the development of student understanding of the organizational sciences: Applications of the canons of the scientific method. Retrieved from http://www.d.umn.edu/~jpierce/Recommendations.pdf

Pinchot, G. III (1985). *Intrapreneurship.* New York: Harper and Row.

Port, M. (2011). *Book yourself solid.* New York: Wiley Publishers.

Porter, L. W., & Lawler, E. E. (1968). *Managerial attitudes and performance.* Homewood, IL: Richard D. Irwin Inc.

Porter, L. W., & Lawler, E. E. (2011). Retrieved September 22, 2011.

Pounds, J. (2006). The great motivational myth. *Management Services 50*(3), 40–44.

Provitera, M. J. (2011). Motivational scholarship: Enlightening, balancing, and transcending traditional approaches. *Academy of Management Annual Meeting.* August 12, 2011. San Antonio, TX.

Quick, T. L. (1980). *The quick motivation method.* St. Martin's Press.

Quinn, R. E. (1996). *Deep change: Discovering the leader within.* San Francisco, CA: Jossey-Bass Inc., p. 74, p. 177.

Raico, R. (2010). *The costs of war: Rethinking Churchill, Part 1.* Retrieved October 16, 2010, from http://www.lewrockwell.com/orig/raico-churchill1.html

Ralph Waldo Emerson quote (2011). Retrieved September 16, 2011, from http://thinkexist.com/quotation/what_lies_behind_us_and_what_lies_before_us_are/10712.html

Raynor, J. O. (1978). *Motivation and career Striving*. In J. W. Atkinson & J. O. Raynor *Personality, motivation, and achievement*. John Wiley & Sons.

Retrieved September 18, 2011, from http://thinkexist.com/quotation/every_morning_in_africa-a_gazelle_wakes_up-it/298139.html.

Robbins, A. (2011). *Tony Robbins asks why we do what we do*. Retrieved September 3, 2011, from http://www.ted.com/talks/tony_robbins_asks_why_we_do_what_we_do.html

Robbins, S. P., & Judge, T. A. (2011). *Organizational Behavior* (14th ed.). Englewood Cliffs, NJ: Prentice-Hall Publishers.

Robins, A. (1992). *Awaken the giant within: How to take immediate control of your mental, emotional, physical, and financial destiny*. Free Press Publishers, p. 24, p. 37.

Rohn, J. (2010). *Cultivating an unshakable character*. Retrieved September 11, 2010, from http://www.jimrohn.com/index.php?main_page=product_info&products_id=910

Rohn, J. (2010). *The major key to your better future is you*. Retrieved September 20, 2010, from http://www.woopidoo.com/articles/jimrohn6success.htm

Rohn, J. (2011). *Cultivating an unshakable character*. Retrieved January 22, 2011, from http://www.jimrohn.com/index.php?main_page=product_info&products_id=910

Romando, R. (2010). *Define motivation*. Retrieved October 8, 2010, from http://EzineArticles.com/?expert=Richard_Romando

Ryan, R. M. (1982). Control and information in the intrapersonal sphere: An extension of cognitive evaluation theory. *Journal of Personality and Social Psychology 48*, 450–461.

Ryan, R. M., & Connell, J. P. (1989). Perceived locus of causality and internationalization: Examining reasons for acting in two domains. *Journal of Personality and Social Psychology 57*, 749–761.

Say, Baptiste, J. (1800). *Entrepreneur defined*. Retrieved October 8, 2010, from http://cn.wikipedia.org/wiki/Entrepreneur

Schwarz and McCarthy, T. (2007). Manage your energy, not your time. *Harvard Business School Press*.

Sedgwick, W. (1888). *Studies from the Biological Laboratory*.

Self Efficacy Site (2011). Retrieved from http://des.emory.edu/mfp/efficacynotgiveup.html

Seligman, M. E. P. (1998). *Learned optimism: How to change your mind and your life*. New York: Free Press.

Seligman, M. E. P. (2004). Happiness interventions that work: the first results. *Authentic Happiness Coaching Newsletter, 2*(10), 1–4.

Shelp, E. (1984). Courage: A neglected virtue in the patient-physician relationship. *Social Science and Medicine 18*, 351–360.

Sificus, S. (2010). *Who was who in the Civil War?* Retrieved October 11, 2010, from http://www.civilwarhome.com/jlchamberlainbio.htm

Simon, H. A. (1955). A behavioral model of rational choice. *Quarterly Journal of Economics 69*, 99–118.

Simon, H. A. (1957). *Models of man—social and rational.* New York: John Wiley & Sons.

Simon, H. A. (1981). *The sciences of the artificial* (2nd ed.). Cambridge, MA: MIT Press.

Simon and Shuster Audio (1980). *Developing winner's habits* (read by Denis Waitley).

Simpson, B. D. (2000). *Ulysses S. Grant: Triumph over adversity, 1822–1865.* Houghton Mifflin Harcourt Publishers.

Soegaard, M. (2011). *Satisficing.* Retrieved July 25, 2011, from http://interaction-design.org/encyclopedia/satisficing.html

Stroebe, W. (2010). The graying of academia: Will it reduce scientific productivity? *American Psychologist 64*(7), 660–673.

Sutcliffe, K. M., & Vogus, T. (2003). *Organizing for resilience.* In K. S. Cameron, J. E. Dutton, & R. E. Quinn (Eds.), *Positive organizational scholarship* (pp. 94–110). San Francisco, CA: Berret-Koehler.

SWOT analysis. (2011). Retrieved September 14, 2011, from http://marketingteacher.com/swot/history-of-swot.html

The Bucket List (movie) (2011). Retrieved September 18, 2011, from http://www.imdb.com/title/tt0825232/

The Calf Path, Sam Walter Foss (written in the late 1800s) (1997). Center for Professional Development and Services, Phi Delta Kappa International.

The Calf's Path by Sam Walter Foss (2011). Writers almanac. Retrieved October 11, 2011, from http://writersalmanac.publicradio.org/index.php?date=2007/06/11

The Frog and the scorpion (2011). Retrieved September 16, 2011, from http://en.wikipedia.org/wiki/The_Scorpion_and_the_Frog

The Geisha Boy (movie) (1958). Retrieved December 31, 2010, from http://www.imdb.com/title/tt0051649/

The Godfather (movie) Retrieved September 15, 2011, from http://www.imdb.com/title/tt0068646/

The Joneses (movie) (2011). Retrieved September 17, 2011, from http://www.imdb.com/title/tt1285309/

Think and Grow Rich. Retrieved September 16, 2011, from http://en.wikipedia.org/wiki/Napoleon_Hill

Thomas, K. W. (2000). *Intrinsic motivation to work: Building energy and commitment.* San Francisco, CA: Berrett-Koehler Publishers Inc, p. 6.

Thomas, K. W., & Tymon, W. G. (1993). *Empowerment inventory.* Consulting. Palo Alto, CA: Psychologist Press.

Thomas, K. W., & Velthouse, B. A. (1990). Cognitive elements of empowerment: An 'interpretive' model of intrinsic task motivation. Academy of Management. *The Academy of Management Review* 15(4), 666.

Tracy, B. (1993). *Maximum achievement: The proven system of strategies and skills that will unlock your hidden powers to succeed*. New York: Simon & Schuster, p. 123.

Tracy, B. (2010). *Mind power: Words of wisdom for positive thinking*. Retrieved September 20, 2010, from http://www.briantracy.com/blog/general/mind-power-words-of-wisdom-for-positive-thinking/#more-1780

Tracy, B. (2010). *The Goals Movie*. Retrieved September 21, 2010, from http://video1.nightingale.com/goals/goalsmovie.html?promo=inthpgoals

Tracy, B. (2010). *The ultimate goals program*. Retrieved September 21, 2010, from http://video1.nightingale.com

Vroom, V. H. (1964). *Work and motivation*. John Wiley & Sons.

Vroom, V. Retrieved September 22, 2011 from http://en.wikipedia.org/wiki/Victor_Vroom

Waitley, D. (2010). *The psychology of winning*. Retrieved September 21, 2010, from http://nightingale.com

Waterman, R. H. (1994). *What America does right: Learning from companies that put people first?* (1st ed.). W. W. Norton & Company.

Weiner, B., Russell, D., & Lerman, D. (1978). Affective consequences of causal ascriptions. In J. H. Harvey, W. J. Ickes, & R. F. Kidd (Eds.), *New directions for attribution research* (Vol. 2, pp. 59–90). Hillsdale, NJ: Erlbaum.

Welch, J. (2011). Retrieved September 15, 2011 from http://www.brainyquote.com/quotes/authors/j/jack_welch.html

Welch, J., & Welch, S. (2005). *Winning*. Harperbusiness Publishers, pp. 4–5.

White, R. C. (2003). *Lincoln's Greatest Speech: The Second Inaugural*. New York: Simon & Schuster.

Winnie the Pooh, Walt Disney Corporation (2011). Retrieved September 23, 2011, from http://en.wikipedia.org/wiki/Winnie-the-Pooh

Woody Allen quote. (2011). Retrieved September 14, 2011 from http://www.quotationspage.com/quote/1903.html

Wren, D. A., & Bedeian, A. G. (2009). *The evolution of management thought* (6th ed.). New York: Wiley Publishers.

Wright, P. (2010). Retrieved September 14, 2010 from http://tribute.jimrohn.com/comments/thanks

Zigler, Z. (2010). *Entrepreneur advice: Why worry*. Retrieved October 17, 2010, from http://www.evancarmichael.com/Entrepreneur-Advice/448/Why-Worry.html

Ziva, K. (1999). *Social cognition: Making sense of people*. Cambridge, MA: MIT Press; (Simon 1957; 1981, as cited in Kunda 1999).

Index

A
Abraham Maslow's need model, 30–32
Acceptance, 13
Achievement-oriented action, 117
Affection, 13
Affirmation, 13
Age-related changes, 114
Agreeableness, 67, 69
Attention, 13
Attentional focus, 73
Authenticity, 6
Authority, 13
Automatic thoughts, 118
Autotelic experience, 58

B
Bonafide geniuses, 85
Bounded rationality, 74
Brain science, 112
Butterfly effect, 86

C
Carrot-and-stick motivation, 59, 113
Cathexis, 62
Change now
    continuous improvement, 103
    Kotter's eight-step change model, 102
    resistance, 100
    unfreeze, change, refreeze, 101
Chastity, 71
Clayton Paul Alderfer's hierarchy, 32–33
Cleanliness, 71
CLIP (clear logical improvements for people), 4
CLOP (control, lead, organize, and plan), 4, 48
Coach, 12
Cognitive fitness, 42
Cognitive-learning effect, 117
Compelling vision, 92
Conscientiousness, 68, 69
Constructive criticism, 62
Content, 44
Continuous improvement, 103
Control, 48

D
Daydreaming, 67, 87
Deming cycle, 103
Direction, variation in, 74
Disappointment, 19
Dream, 48

E
Economic downturn, 87
Effective leaders, 14
Emotional intelligence, 62
Empowering yourself, 60–63
Entity theory, 18
Entrepreneur, intrapreneur, motrapreneur, 10–12
Equity theory, 91, 117
ERG (existence, relatedness, and growth) theory, 32
Expectancy theory, 44–46, 117
External locus, 67, 68
Extraversion, 68, 69, 81
Extrinsic motivation, 37
Extrinsic rewards, 38, 42, 57, 58, 113–115

F
Five personality traits, 68, 81
Flow experience, 58
Flow, 58, 62, 64
Force field analysis, 90, 101
Fringe benefits, 15
Frugality, 71

INDEX

G
Goal setting, 17
Goals, learning, 17
Great American leaders, 69–72

H
Happiness, 17
Happy, 15
Hedonic calculus, 21
Herzberg's two-factor theory, 60, 63
Human capital, 116
Human potential movement, 78
Human relations movement, 15, 77
Hygiene, 58

I
Ignoring conflict, 15
Immediate-motivator effect, 117
Incentive, 44
Incremental theory, 18
Individual behaviour, 21
Industry, 71
Intelligence quotient (IQ), 42
Intelligence, 15, 18
Intensity, 74
Internal locus, 67, 81, 111
Intrinsic motivation, 58, 115, 119
Intrinsic rewards, 57, 62, 113

J
Job participation, 16
Justice, 71

K
Kaizen, 11
Kotter's eight-step change model, 102

L
Lead, 48
Life stages, 115
Lifelong learning, 75
Long-range objectives, 100

M
Maslow, Mcdougall, and Maltz on motivation, 72
Maslow's hierarchy of needs, 30, 58, 117

Mediocrity of the masses, 77
Miraculous birth, 90
Moderation, 71
Modus operandi, 90
Money, 15
Moral or ethical honor, 62
Motivation
  definition, 10
  entrepreneur, intrapreneur, motrapreneur, 10–12
  motivation and ability, 20
  motivation breakthrough, 18–20
  motivation myths, 14–16
  personal SWOT analysis, 16
  perspectives, 17
Motivation and ability, 20
Motivation breakthrough, 18–20
Motivation myths, 14–16
Motivation need management
  Abraham Maslow's need model, 30–32
  Clayton Paul Alderfer's hierarchy, 32–33
Motivational force theory, 45
Motivational mind-set, 3–6
Motivators, 58, 63
Motrapreneur, 21

N
Need theory, 30
Negative emotions, 43
Neologism, 74
Neural pathways, 101
Neuroticism, 68
New shapes, giants with, 78–80

O
Openness to experience, 68–69, 81
Oratory skills, 70
Order, 71
Organizational behavior field, 87
Organize, 48
Outer life, 72

P
Peer-controlled pay system, 77
Performance goals, 17, 20
Perseverance, 11

Persistence, 74
Personal
  change, 61, 102
  equity, 91
  excellence, 116–118
  SWOT analysis, 16
Personality, your, 67–69
Perspectives, 17
Pessimistic reveries, 78
Peter principle, 113
Plan, 48
Plan, do, check, and act, 103
Planning, 43, 49, 73, 75, 83
Popular psychology, 78
Positive organizational behavior, 86–89
Positive psychology, 47–49
  butterflies, 86
  compelling vision, 92
  equity theory, 91
  positive organizational behavior, 86–89
  purposeful life, 90
  scholars, motivational and self-help, 89
Process theory, 44
Psychic energy, 62
Psycho-cybernetics, 72
Psychological capital, 81, 86–88
Punishment, 16
Purposeful life, 90

R
Refreezing, 100
Reinventing yourself
  brain science, 112
  reward systems, 112
Relationships, 78, 81, 93, 113
Resistance, 100
Resolution, 71
Responsibilities, 74, 114
Reticular activating system (RAS), 73
Reward system, 10, 112

S
Satisfice, 74
Scholars, motivational and self-help, 89

Self-actualization, 31, 33, 58, 71, 75, 116
Self-development, 81, 94
Self-efficacy, 49
Self-esteem, 18, 31, 100
Self-guided purpose, 6
Self-image, 72
Self-leadership and motivation, 41, 46
  expectancy theory, 44–46
  leading yourself, 46
  positive psychology, 47–49
  process theory, 44
  self-efficacy, 49
  taking control, 42–44
Self-motivation, 1, 11, 15, 21, 22, 31, 34, 44, 45, 50, 63, 87, 92, 102, 112, 115, 116, 118, 119
Shaping, 75
Short-term goals, 100
Silence, 70
Sincerity, 71
Social media, 24–25
Social, 44
Spontaneity, 73
Strengths, your
  empowering yourself, 60–63
  intrinsic motivation, 58
  two-factor theory of motivation, 58
Success, 58, 116
Swarm intelligence, 14
SWOT (strengths, weaknesses, opportunities, and threats), 16, 21

T
Temperance, 70
Theory X, 76, 77
Theory Y, 76–78
Theory X and Y, 76
Totality of reaction, 75
Tranquility, 71
Transpersonal motives, 3
Trauma, 61
Turbulent environment, 87
Twelve-step system, 81
Two-factor theory of motivation, 58

U
Unfreeze, 100
Unfreeze, change, refreeze, 101
Upward mobility, 74

Y
Yourself, believing in
  great American leaders, 69–72
  human relations movement, 77
  Maslow, McDougall, and Maltz on motivation, 72
  new shapes, giants with, 78–80
  shoulders of giants, 72–76
  theory X and Y, 76
  your personality, 67–69
yourself, leading, 46

OTHER TITLES IN OUR HUMAN RESOURCE MANAGEMENT AND ORGANIZATIONAL BEHAVIOR COLLECTION

Jean Phillips, Rutgers University and Stan Gully, Rutgers University, Collection Editors

- *Career Management* by Donald Vijay Sathe
- *Developing Employee Talent to Perform* by Kim Warren
- *Performance Management* by Joseph McCune
- *Conducting Performance Appraisals* by Michael Gordon and Vernon Miller
- *Culturally Intelligent Leadership: Leading Through Intercultural Interactions* by Mai Moua
- *Letting People Go: The People-Centered Approach to Firing and Laying Off Employees* by Matt Shlosberg
- *Negotiating and Defending Your Margin* by Philippe Korda
- *Managing Employee Turnover: Myths to Dispel and Strategies for Effective Management* by David Allen and Phil Bryant
- *Cross-Cultural Management* by Veronica Velo
- *How to Coach Individuals, Teams and Organizations to Master Transformational Change: Surfing Tsunamis* by Stephen K. Hacker

Announcing the Business Expert Press Digital Library

Concise E-books Business Students Need for Classroom and Research

This book can also be purchased in an e-book collection by your library as
- a one-time purchase,
- that is owned forever,
- allows for simultaneous readers,
- has no restrictions on printing, and
- can be downloaded as PDFs from within the library community.

Our digital library collections are a great solution to beat the rising cost of textbooks. e-books can be loaded into their course management systems or onto student's e-book readers.

The **Business Expert Press** digital libraries are very affordable, with no obligation to buy in future years. For more information, please visit www.businessexpertpress.com/librarians. To set up a trial in the United States, please contact **Adam Chesler** at *adam.chesler@businessexpertpress.com* for all other regions, contact **Nicole Lee** at *nicole.lee@igroupnet.com*.

www.ingramcontent.com/pod-product-compliance
Lightning Source LLC
Chambersburg PA
CBHW070550170426
43201CB00012B/1792